History Of Japan

A Journey Through Japanese History

(Exploring The Craftsmanship And Legacy Of Japan's Artisanal Dolls)

Jewel Burns

Published By **Hailey Leigh**

Jewel Burns

History Of Japan: A Journey Through Japanese History (Exploring The Craftsmanship And Legacy Of Japan's Artisanal Dolls)

ISBN 978-1-7781462-6-8

No part of this guidebook shall be reproduced in any form without permission in writing from the publisher except in the case of brief quotations embodied in critical articles or reviews.

Legal & Disclaimer

The information contained in this book is not designed to replace or take the place of any form of medicine or professional medical advice. The information in this book has been provided for educational & entertainment purposes only.

The information contained in this book has been compiled from sources deemed reliable, and it is accurate to the best of the Author's knowledge; however, the Author cannot guarantee its accuracy and validity and cannot be held liable for any errors or omissions. Changes are periodically made to this book. You must consult your doctor or get professional medical advice before using any of the suggested remedies, techniques, or information in this book.

Upon using the information contained in this book, you agree to hold harmless the Author from and against any damages, costs, and expenses, including any legal fees potentially resulting from the application of any of the information provided by this guide. This disclaimer applies to any damages or injury caused by the use and application, whether directly or indirectly, of any advice or information presented, whether for breach of contract, tort, negligence, personal injury, criminal intent, or under any other cause of action.

You agree to accept all risks of using the information presented inside this book. You need to consult a professional medical practitioner in order to ensure you are both able and healthy enough to participate in this program.

Table Of Contents

Chapter 1: The Dawn Of Ancient Japan

In the depths of Japanese facts, there exists a wondrous era known as the Jomon period, which serves because of the truth the genesis of ancient Japanese civilization this charming bankruptcy, spanning approximately from 10,000 BCE to three hundred BCE, brims with a rich cultural and innovative records that keeps inspiring awe to in recent times.

The term "Jomon" derives from the best of a type pottery produced throughout this era. These earthenware vessels have been embellished with complicated cord-marked designs, showcasing the fantastic innovative sensibility of the Jomon people. These professional artisans not most effective crafted mind-blowing ceramics but also expressed their creativity through stone and clay sculptures, weaving a tapestry of innovative expression that transcended time.

The Jomon period became characterized with the aid of a semi-sedentary way of life, in which communities lived in small settlements and relied closely on fishing, searching, and gathering for sustenance. Their dwellings can be decided along the coastlines and rivers, deeply interconnected with the natural global that surrounded them. These innovative companies evolved an intimate dating with nature, shaping their daily lives and perception structures.

In addition to their creative achievements, the Jomon humans left inside the back of an array of archaeological treasures that provide glimpses into their everyday lifestyles. Excavations have unearthed stone gadget, weaving implements, rings, and even human collectible figurines, all of which shed mild on the Jomon way of life.

These discoveries imply a society with profound information of their environment, harnessing its assets for survival and expression.

One of the great elements of the Jomon manner of existence is its sturdiness, spanning severa millennia. During this time, the Jomon people experienced numerous cultural shifts and modifications, adapting to the changing landscapes and influences from neighboring areas. It is plain that the Jomon length served as a crucible for the formation of the perfect Japanese identification, laying the inspiration for the subsequent eras of Japanese information.

To definitely understand the Jomon duration is to immerse oneself within the enigmatic beauty of their creative creations, to surprise at their complex pottery, and to contemplate the deep connection they cast with nature. The legacy of the Jomon length resonates within the hearts of the Japanese humans, a testament to the long-lasting spirit of historic Japan that keeps to inspire and captivate. Let us embark in this journey of exploration, as we unveil the mysteries and feature a laugh the vibrant tapestry of the Jomon duration, an technology that holds the key to information the origins of Japan's fantastic cultural statistics.

Divine Origins: Mythology and Creation Stories

In the tapestry of historic Japan's rich cultural historic beyond, mythology and introduction memories maintain a totally particular location. These historic reminiscences provide a glimpse into the beliefs and imagination of the Japanese humans, weaving a tale of divine origins and the complex courting among gods, nature, and humanity. Let us delve into the arena of historical Japanese mythology and find out the captivating memories that formed the non secular landscape of the land of the growing solar.

At the coronary heart of Japanese mythology lies the Kojiki, meaning "Record of Ancient Matters," and the Nihon Shoki, moreover known as "The Chronicles of Japan." These ancient texts, compiled inside the 8th century CE, meticulously chronicle the origins of Japan and its imperial lineage, further to a plethora of charming myths and legends which have been passed down thru generations.

One of the maximum famous myths is the tale of Izanagi and Izanami, the divine couple credited with the appearance of Japan. Legend has it that they stood upon the "floating bridge of heaven" and stirred the primordial sea with a jeweled spear. As the droplets fell again into the water, the islands of Japan have been commonplace. From this union, a pantheon of gods and goddesses emerged, governing severa additives of nature and human life.

Among the divine beings in Japanese mythology, the solar goddess Amaterasu holds a function of terrific significance. She is believed to be the ancestor of the Japanese imperial line and the deity of the solar, radiating slight and presenting lifestyles-giving electricity to the arena. The story of Amaterasu's retreat into a cave, causing darkness and chaos till she emerge as enticed to emerge, symbolizes the cyclical nature of light and darkness and the significance of harmony within the global.

Another prominent deity is Susanoo, the hurricane god and brother of Amaterasu. Known for his turbulent and unpredictable nature, Susanoo's exploits frequently delivered about calamity, however he completed a critical role in shaping the natural international. His battles toward big creatures and his adventure to the underworld replicate the everlasting warfare amongst order and chaos, a topic that resonates deeply in Japanese mythology.

The mythology of historical Japan is replete with captivating testimonies of gods and goddesses, supernatural creatures, and epic battles. These memories no longer only entertained however also served to supply moral classes, societal values, and the interaction among human beings and the divine. They fostered a profound reverence for nature, because of the fact the elements had been frequently personified and imbued with non secular importance.

Throughout the a while, the ones myths have advocated numerous aspects of Japanese subculture, from paintings and literature to spiritual practices and festivals. Shinto, the indigenous faith of Japan, attracts carefully from the myths and rituals surrounding the ones divine beings. Shrines devoted to precise deities dot the landscape, serving as sacred regions wherein humans pays homage and are on the lookout for advantages.

The richness of Japanese mythology continues to captivate and encourage, providing a glimpse into the collective imagination of historical Japan. These myths remind us of the deep non secular connection among humanity and the natural international, and the significance of locating harmony indoors ourselves and with the universe.

Shaping the Land: Agriculture and the Yayoi Culture

In the colourful tapestry of historic Japan, a period of tremendous transformation emerged referred to as the Yayoi way of life. During this period, which spanned from about three hundred BCE to a few hundred CE, the Japanese humans skilled huge improvements in agriculture, all the time shaping the land and laying the idea for the rural practices that would keep the united states of america for hundreds of years to return. Let us adventure lower again to this pivotal time and feature a laugh the long-lasting legacy of the Yayoi way of life.

The Yayoi duration derives its call from the Yayoi district in Tokyo, in which the unique pottery and artifacts of this era had been first excavated. It come to be a time of transition, marked through way of the appearance of wetland rice cultivation and the emergence of settled farming communities. The cultivation of rice, a staple crop that would come to define Japanese cuisine and society, converted the panorama and revolutionized the manner of life for the human beings of ancient Japan.

During the Yayoi period, the Japanese human beings began out to growth present day-day agricultural strategies, which encompass the development of paddy fields. These fields had been cautiously designed to govern water flow, taking into consideration the cultivation of rice in flooded situations. This current technique substantially prolonged agricultural productivity and paved the manner for surplus meals manufacturing, allowing the increase of large settlements and the mounted order of social hierarchies.

With the appearance of settled agriculture, corporations started out to form around agricultural facilities, fostering the increase of interconnected societies. These settlements featured wooden houses extended on stilts, called raised-ground dwellings, which covered them from flooding and allowed for air flow. The improvement of these businesses no longer tremendous facilitated agricultural practices but also gave upward thrust to extra complicated social structures and cultural exchange.

The Yayoi life-style became no longer constrained to agriculture on my own; it also witnessed advancements in metallurgy and the emergence of 1-of-a-kind bronze and iron equipment. These upgrades revolutionized farming techniques and enabled the cultivation of recent vegetation. Iron device, particularly, performed a important role within the clearance of forests, the development of irrigation systems, and the training of land for farming.

In addition to their agricultural prowess, the Yayoi people engaged in colorful creative expressions. The pottery of this era exhibited swish and stylish paperwork, frequently adorned with hard geometric styles and motifs inspired via using nature. These vessels served not best practical functions however moreover symbolized the cultural identification and aesthetic sensibilities of the Yayoi people.

The Yayoi manner of existence completed a important function in laying the inspiration for the following intervals of Japanese history. The agricultural improvements and social systems mounted all through this period fashioned the idea for the improvement of feudal Japan and the samurai warrior magnificence. The enduring legacy of the Yayoi way of life may be seen within the endured cultivation of rice and the reverence for the land that remains ingrained in Japanese society to at the present time.

Chapter 2: The Birth Of A Centralized Government

In the annals of historic Japan's storied records, a super financial disaster unfolds with the upward push of the Yamato Dynasty. This generation marks a momentous duration of political and cultural improvement, because the Yamato extended family laid the muse for a centralized government that could form the future of Japan for loads of destiny years. Let us embark on a journey to find out the transport of a centralized authorities and function fun the enduring legacy of the Yamato Dynasty.

The origins of the Yamato Dynasty can be traced back to the third century CE, while the Yamato prolonged family emerged as a distinguished strength inside the Yamato vicinity, this is gift-day Nara Prefecture. Through astute political maneuvering and strategic alliances, the Yamato prolonged circle of relatives step by step extended their have an effect on and consolidated their authority over neighboring areas.

Under the management of the Yamato rulers, a centralized government began to take form, marking a departure from the fragmented tribal governance that had prevailed in in advance instances. The Yamato court docket docket set up itself because the political and cultural center, drawing idea from the political structures of neighboring nations, especially China and Korea. This have an effect on, coupled with indigenous customs and traditions, fostered the perfect man or woman of the Yamato authorities.

The Yamato rulers applied a device of hereditary succession, with the imperial throne passing from one era to the following in the ruling clan. This set up a enjoy of balance and continuity, presenting a framework for governance and the development of a workplace work to manage the affairs of the kingdom. The imperial court have grow to be a picture of authority, serving as the focus for political selection-making and the embodiment of Japan's country wide identification.

During this era, the Yamato Dynasty faced various annoying conditions and conflicts, both internally and externally. They encountered rival factions inner their private extended own family, vying for strength and influence. Additionally, the Yamato court docket had to take care of close by chieftains and nearby tribes trying to find to claim their autonomy. These struggles for dominance and group spirit commonplace the political landscape of ancient Japan and brought on the Yamato rulers to adopt diplomatic techniques to hold balance.

The Yamato Dynasty additionally solid critical alliances with neighboring global locations, in particular Korea and China, facilitating cultural exchanges and introducing new technology and thoughts to Japan. The adoption of Chinese writing systems, Buddhist teachings, and Confucian standards recommended the governance, control, and social fabric of historical Japan. This circulate-pollination of cultures enriched the Yamato court docket docket's repertoire of facts and contributed to the development of a complex society.

Under the Yamato Dynasty, the Yamato court docket docket sought to solidify their authority via manner of promoting a feel of concord and shared identification a number of the severa regions of Japan. They fostered the mixture of community customs and ideals into the growing national popularity, spotting the importance of preserving social concord and collective concord. This inclusive technique allowed for the coexistence of numerous ethnic corporations and facilitated the integration of different cultural factors right proper right into a extremely good Japanese identity.

The start of a centralized government beneath the Yamato Dynasty laid the concept for the following eras of Japanese statistics. The institution of a sturdy imperial courtroom docket, the hooked up order of a bureaucratic tool, and the pursuit of diplomatic circle of relatives individuals with neighboring powers set the diploma for the improvement of a unified Japan. The legacy of the Yamato Dynasty endures in the imperial lineage that maintains to in recent times, symbolizing the historic continuity of Japan's centralized governance.

The Way of the Warrior: Samurai and Bushido

In the annals of historic Japan's storied history, the determine of the samurai stands as an embodiment of honor, loyalty, and martial prowess. The samurai, with their unwavering commitment to a code of behavior known as Bushido, commonplace the cultural landscape of ancient Japan and left an indelible mark at the nation's identity. Let us embark on a adventure to discover the way of the warrior, celebrating the noble spirit of the samurai and the undying thoughts of Bushido.

The samurai emerged in the path of the Heian period (794-1185 CE), despite the fact that their origins may be traced returned to earlier instances. Originally, they served as hooked up warriors, dependable protectors of the noble class, and guardians of the imperial court docket. Over time, their function expanded to embody military and administrative duties, as they have end up an influential elegance that wielded widespread electricity and formed the direction of Japanese records.

At the middle of the samurai ethos come to be Bushido, which may be translated as "the way of the warrior." Bushido encompassed a tough and rapid of ethical requirements, virtues, and moral codes that guided the conduct and behavior of the samurai. These thoughts emphasized unwavering loyalty, braveness in the face of adversity, strength of mind, and an unwavering strength of will to responsibility. It have become a code that not great governed their movements at the battlefield but permeated each detail of their lives.

Central to Bushido end up the idea of loyalty, called "chugi." The samurai pledged unwavering allegiance to their lords, putting the pursuits in their masters above their personal. Loyalty grow to be considered the cornerstone of the samurai's honor, and a breach of this agree with changed into deemed the maximum shame. It changed right right into a bond cast thru mutual understand, and the samurai have been prepared to sacrifice their lives inside the carrier in their lords.

Courage, called "yuuki," become some different virtue held in immoderate esteem via the samurai. They were skilled from a young age to face adversity and meet demanding situations with unwavering bravery. The samurai lived with the know-how that lack of lifestyles in struggle come to be a high-quality possibility, and that they embraced this fact with a peaceful splendor, finding solace inside the information that an honorable loss of life became best to a life with out honor.

Discipline and power of will were instilled inside the samurai through rigorous education and the pursuit of mastery in the martial arts. They honed their capabilities in numerous fight techniques, which includes archery, swordsmanship, and horsemanship. The pursuit of perfection in the ones arts grow to be now not in reality for self-gratification however a manner to cultivate undertaking, hobby, and intellectual fortitude.

Beyond their martial prowess, the samurai had been clients of the humanities, fostering a wealthy cultural legacy. They embraced poetry, calligraphy, tea rite, and flower arranging, seeing them as critical additives of a properly-rounded education. The samurai's appreciation for aesthetics and refinement balanced their warrior nature, exemplifying the concord between the humanities and martial virtues.

The legacy of the samurai and Bushido extended past the battlefield. Their have an effect on permeated the social fabric of historical Japan, shaping notions of honor, integrity, and social order. The samurai had been no longer top notch warriors but moreover administrators, educators, and guardians of justice. They maintained peace and stability inner their domains, making sure the nicely-being of the corporations they served.

The samurai spirit endures in modern-day Japan, serving as a supply of notion and a reminder of the noble values that cross beyond time. The standards of Bushido preserve to resonate, guiding people of their pursuit of private increase, integrity, and honor. The samurai legacy remains an crucial part of Japan's cultural identification, symbolizing the indomitable spirit of historical Japan and the enduring quest for excellence.

Building Bridges: Cultural Exchange with China and Korea

In the colourful tapestry of ancient Japan's cultural historic past, the threads of connection and exchange with neighboring civilizations weave a story of boom, enrichment, and mutual idea. The bridges that have been constructed through cultural alternate with China and Korea allowed historic Japan to consist of recent thoughts, era, and innovative expressions, leaving an indelible mark at the state's identification. Let us embark on a journey to explore the profound have an impact on of China and Korea on ancient Japan, celebrating the electricity of move-cultural fertilization.

The cultural trade amongst ancient Japan and China flourished for the duration of the Asuka (592-710 CE) and Nara (710-794 CE) periods, characterised with the useful resource of an influx of mind, facts, and spiritual ideals from the Chinese mainland. The transmission of Buddhism, Confucianism, and Taoism to Japan had a profound impact, reshaping spiritual and philosophical landscapes and introducing new procedures of wondering.

Buddhism, specifically, finished a pivotal characteristic inside the cultural exchange amongst Japan and China. It arrived in Japan thru Korean kingdoms, which includes Baekje and Goguryeo, which had established near ties with China. The teachings of Buddhism resonated deeply with the Japanese human beings, presenting solace, non secular guidance, and a new lens through which to recognize the area. Buddhist temples, statues, and sutras became an essential part of Japanese spiritual existence and progressive expression.

The affect of Chinese culture extended beyond religion. Chinese writing systems, referred to as kanji, were delivered to Japan, becoming the muse of the written language. Chinese literature, philosophy, and administrative structures additionally decided their manner into the material of Japanese society, enriching highbrow discourse and shaping the governing systems.

Furthermore, the art work forms of China, inclusive of painting, calligraphy, and shape, left an indelible mark on Japan. The aesthetic sensibilities of historical China inspired Japanese artists and craftsmen, who tailored and diffused the ones impacts to create their particular inventive expressions. The splendor of Chinese ink painting, the grace of calligraphic strokes, and the architectural varieties of temples and palaces prompted the development of Japanese paintings and shape.

Alongside China, Korea served as a important bridge for cultural exchange with historical Japan. The kingdoms of Baekje, Goguryeo, and Silla established robust diplomatic and change individuals of the circle of relatives with Japan, facilitating the drift of thoughts, generation, and cultural practices. These connections fostered a dynamic alternate in various fields, on the facet of agriculture, structure, governance, and the arts.

Korean artisans and craftsmen done a large feature in the improvement of Japanese ceramics, mainly at some stage in the Kofun (250-538 CE) and Asuka durations. The Korean peninsula modified into renowned for its superior pottery techniques, and this understanding changed into eagerly embraced and tailored through Japanese potters. The ensuing fusion of Korean and Japanese styles gave birth to top notch pottery traditions, which consist of Sue ware and Haji ware.

The cultural alternate with China and Korea no longer top notch enriched Japan's innovative and highbrow landscapes but moreover stimulated improvements in era and governance. Knowledge of Chinese irrigation structures, agricultural practices, and engineering techniques contributed to the development of infrastructure, enhancing agricultural productivity and shaping Japan's panorama.

The trade of mind and cultural practices amongst historic Japan, China, and Korea turned into no longer a one-sided affair. Japan, too, shared its unique customs, artwork office paintings, and technologies, contributing to the collective cultural wealth of the place. This reciprocal trade fostered a experience of interconnectedness and mutual appreciation, laying the basis for destiny collaborations and shared legacies.

They have an impact on of China and Korea on historic Japan stays obvious inside the gift-day, serving as a testament to the iconic strength of cultural change. The shared information and shared cultural historical past bind those global locations together, celebrating the high-quality capability of human societies to test from every other and evolve in harmony.

Chapter 3: The Influence Of Buddhism

In the serene landscapes of historical Japan, a profound non secular way of life took root, remodeling the hearts and minds of its human beings. The teachings of Buddhism, mainly the Zen college, permeated the cultural material of Japan and left an indelible mark on its imaginative expression, philosophical discourse, and pursuit of enlightenment. Let us embark on a journey to find out the profound have an effect on of Buddhism, celebrating the transformative strength of Zen and its enduring legacy in historical Japan.

Buddhism become introduced to Japan in the sixth century CE, making its manner from the Korean peninsula and the neighboring kingdoms of Baekje, Goguryeo, and Silla. As the training unfold, they resonated deeply with the Japanese human beings, presenting solace, understanding, and a route to religious liberation. Buddhism, with its emphasis on compassion, the impermanence of life, and the individual of suffering, supplied a profound framework for expertise the human state of affairs.

Within Buddhism, the Zen faculty, referred to as "Chan" in China, finished a pivotal function in shaping the religious landscape of historic Japan. Zen emphasised direct revel in and intuitive notion, encouraging practitioners to go beyond intellectual expertise and delve into direct consciousness of one's actual nature. It provided a path to enlightenment that transcended spiritual dogma and ritual, emphasizing an instantaneous, experiential technique to awakening.

Zen teachings were deeply brought on with the aid of the classes of Indian Buddhism, specially the Mahayana manner of existence. The standards of "emptiness" (shunyata) and "interdependent origination" (pratityasamutpada) formed the philosophical foundation of Zen, hard practitioners to question the person of fact and the illusory nature of the self. These teachings sparked a radical shift in perception, urging humans to domesticate a proper away revel in of the prevailing second.

One of the hallmarks of Zen workout is the art work of meditation, called zazen. Sitting in stillness, Zen practitioners are attempting to find to quiet the mind and cultivate a country of alert, non-discriminating attention. Through sustained exercising, they try and move beyond dualistic questioning and hook up with the essence of existence. Zazen have emerge as the cornerstone of Zen training, presenting a pathway to perception and the direct revel in of one's inherent Buddha nature.

The impact of Zen prolonged a long manner beyond the geographical areas of non secular exercising. Its impact permeated severa elements of Japanese manner of existence, leaving an indelible mark on artwork, poetry, architecture, and the tea rite. Zen aesthetics emphasized simplicity, minimalism, and an appreciation for the beauty of imperfection. This aesthetic sensibility, called "wabi-sabi," celebrated the quick nature of life and the inherent splendor observed inside the imperfect, the aged, and the u . S ..

The Zen garden, with its carefully prepared rocks, raked gravel, and meticulously positioned factors, have end up a picture of meditative reflected picture and a manifestation of the Zen philosophy inside the physical international. These gardens have been designed to awaken a sense of serenity, inviting contemplation and a deep reference to nature. They served as a seen expression of the interaction among stillness and motion, form and formlessness.

The tea rite, stimulated through way of Zen requirements, became a ritualized exercising embodying mindfulness and the appreciation of simplicity. It emphasized the importance of being in truth discovered in every second, treating every movement with reverence and hobby to element. The tea rite served as a automobile for religious communion, bringing together host and traveler in a shared experience of grace, concord, and calmness.

The have an effect on of Buddhism, particularly Zen, on historic Japan become profound. It reshaped the religious landscape, presenting a direction to enlightenment that transcended spiritual boundaries. The teachings of Zen challenged traditional wondering, inspiring people to searching out direct revel in and have interaction in self-inquiry. The creative expressions inspired thru Zen maintain to inspire, reminding us of the profound splendor and knowledge located in simplicity, imperfection, and the triumphing second.

Courtly Elegance: Heian Period and the Tale of Genji

In the spell binding realm of historical Japan, a length of subtle beauty spread out, called the Heian duration. It modified right into a time of top notch beauty, complex courtly rituals, and a flourishing literary manner of life that produced one of the global's best literary works, the Tale of Genji. Let us embark on a adventure to the resplendent worldwide of the Heian period, celebrating its courtly beauty and the iconic legacy of the Tale of Genji.

The Heian length spanned from 794 to 1185 CE, named after the capital town of Heian-kyō, gift-day Kyoto. During this era, the aristocratic class flourished, growing a complicated and considerably diffused way of life that centered across the imperial court docket docket. The nobility, called the Kuge, immersed themselves in inventive hobbies, poetry, track, and glossy courtly rituals.

At the heart of Heian courtroom way of life became the pursuit of beauty and aesthetic refinement. The courtiers sought to create an environment of subtle splendor, wherein artwork, poetry, and literature thrived. They cultivated an appreciation for nature's subtle splendor, cherishing the fleeting moments of the converting seasons. This aesthetic sensibility, known as "miyabi," celebrated grace, subtlety, and understated elegance.

One of the crowning achievements of the Heian duration turned into the Tale of Genji, written with the resource of Lady Murasaki Shikibu, a female-in-geared up on the court docket. This masterpiece, composed across the early 11th century, is often appeared as the sector's first novel. It follows the life and romantic encounters of Hikaru Genji, a nobleman, capturing the hard nuances of courtly life, love, and human emotions.

The Tale of Genji stands as a testomony to the literary sophistication of the Heian length. Lady Murasaki's poetic prose and lyrical descriptions painted outstanding images of courtly lifestyles, taking pix the subtleties of emotions, and delving into the complexities of human relationships. It showcased the courtly rituals, the sensitive courtship practices, and the poetic exchanges that fashioned the tapestry of Heian court docket lifestyle.

The Heian court docket turned into famend for its complex rituals and ceremonies. Courtiers engaged in complex dances, song performances, and poetry competitions, seeking out to illustrate their refinement and wit. These cultural interests have been no longer really leisure sports activities however a way of social interaction, expression, and showcasing one's cultural acumen.

Poetry held a completely unique vicinity in Heian court docket docket way of lifestyles. Refined courtiers engaged in the composition of tanka and waka poetry, which found strict regulations of syllable depend and shape. The artwork of composing poetry have become a vehicle for self-expression, emotional exploration, and a way to talk one's thoughts and feelings in an stylish and touchy way.

The Heian period changed into additionally a time of vibrant creative expression.

Lavish court docket clothing, referred to as "juni-hitoe," adorned the nobility, showcasing hard layers of colourful gowns and symbolic accessories. Visual arts, which includes portray and calligraphy, flourished, with artists employing touchy brushwork and capturing the ethereal beauty of nature.

Within the Heian courtroom docket, ladies performed a huge function in cultural and literary circles. They were substantially knowledgeable and actively participated in creative interests. Lady Murasaki Shikibu, as exemplified thru her authorship of the Tale of Genji, stands as a testament to the literary skills and highbrow prowess of girls within the course of this period.

The Heian length became not without its demanding conditions and political intrigues. The courtroom docket docket became regularly embroiled in power struggles, and the impact of noble families waxed and waned. However, amidst the ones fluctuations, the subtle court docket subculture thrived, leaving an indelible mark at the cultural history of Japan.

The legacy of the Heian duration and the Tale of Genji endures inside the hearts and minds of the Japanese humans. It represents a golden age of courtly beauty, in which artwork, literature, and delicate manners were loved and celebrated. The Tale of Genji remains a undying masterpiece, shooting the essence of human emotions and the intricacies of courtly lifestyles.

The Rise of the Shogun: Kamakura and the Minamoto Clan

In the annals of ancient Japan, a transformative era spread out with the upward thrust of the samurai warrior beauty and the hooked up order of the Kamakura shogunate. This period, marked via the ascendancy of the Minamoto prolonged family, heralded a modern-day-day technology of navy rule and commonplace the path of Japanese information. Let us embark on a journey to discover the upward push of the shogun, celebrating the indomitable spirit of the Minamoto extended family and the enduring legacy of the Kamakura duration.

The Kamakura length spanned from 1185 to 1333 CE, named after the city of Kamakura, which served because the political middle of energy. During this time, Japan witnessed a shift in governance, as real energy shifted from the imperial courtroom to the military elite. The Minamoto prolonged circle of relatives, led via Minamoto no Yoritomo, emerged powerful inside the Genpei War, a war that pitted them towards the rival Taira extended own family.

Minamoto no Yoritomo, a powerful military chief, installation the Kamakura shogunate, making him the number one shogun in Japanese information. The shogun, that means "desired," held de facto political strength, at the equal time as the emperor retained a symbolic function. The establishment of the shogunate marked a massive departure from the centralized authorities of the preceding eras, as military leaders assumed authority and created a ultra-current machine of governance.

Under the Kamakura shogunate, the samurai warrior beauty have emerge as the backbone of political power and navy rule. The samurai, with their unwavering loyalty, martial skills, and adherence to the code of Bushido, served because the shogun's depended on vassals and protectors. They shaped the warrior aristocracy, wielding massive have an effect on and shaping the social cloth of ancient Japan.

The upward thrust of the shogun delivered about a reorganization of the authorities form. The united states emerge as divided into navy provinces, each governed with the resource of a military real appointed with the resource of the usage of the shogun. This decentralized tool allowed for additonal autonomy the diverse neighborhood army leaders, called daimyo, who held big power and administered their domains.

The Kamakura length moreover witnessed the development of a considered one of a type warrior way of life. The samurai embraced martial arts, collectively with archery, swordsmanship, and horsemanship, as a manner of honing their capabilities and embodying the spirit of Bushido. They cultivated a strict code of behavior that emphasized loyalty, honor, and scenario. These values permeated every factor of samurai lifestyles, defining their social fame and shaping their interactions with society.

The Kamakura length became now not without its demanding conditions. The Mongol invasions, led with the resource of Kublai Khan within the overdue 13th century, posed a vast chance to Japan. The samurai, underneath the management of the shogunate, correctly repelled the invaders in crucial Mongol invasions, referred to as the Mongol Invasions of Japan. These conflicts further solidified the army prowess and resilience of the samurai warrior elegance.

The Kamakura length is also related to the emergence of Zen Buddhism as a high-quality non secular way of life. Zen teachings, with their emphasis on direct enjoy and intuitive notion, resonated deeply with the samurai and induced their approach to martial arts and the pursuit of enlightenment. Zen monasteries, together with Kenchoji and Engakuji, have come to be centers of spiritual workout and cultural alternate.

The legacy of the Kamakura duration endures within the cultural and historic material of Japan. The repute quo of the shogunate laid the muse for future navy governments, shaping the trajectory of Japanese feudalism. The samurai ethos, cultivated at some stage in this era, maintains to encourage notions of honor, loyalty, and trouble. The Kamakura duration serves as a testament to the indomitable spirit of the Minamoto prolonged family and their enduring impact at the course of Japanese records.

Chapter 4: The Mongol Invasions

In the annals of ancient Japan, a chapter unfolds that celebrates the resilience and bravado of a kingdom united towards the ambitious Mongol invasions. These invasions, led with the useful resource of Kublai Khan within the past due thirteenth century, posed a sizeable threat to Japan's sovereignty, however the unwavering spirit and strategic protection measures of the Japanese people prevailed. Let us embark on a adventure to find out the battles and defenses of the Mongol invasions, celebrating the indomitable spirit of ancient Japan.

The Mongol invasions of Japan, known as the Mongol Invasions of Japan, passed off in 1274 and 1281 CE. These invasions were a part of Kublai Khan's grand desires to increase his empire and exert dominance over neighboring lands. The Mongol forces, with their large armies and naval prowess, posed an fantastic chance to the sovereignty of Japan.

The first Mongol invasion, referred to as the First Mongol Invasion, came about in 1274. A fleet of approximately 900 ships wearing an expected 23,000 Mongol, Chinese, and Korean infantrymen set sail in the direction of Japan's beaches. Their target have turn out to be the island of Kyushu, domestic to strategic ports and towns.

The Japanese forces, led with the aid of samurai warriors and nearby lords, prepared for the imminent invasion. They recognized the significance of the chance and mobilized their defenses as a end result. The samurai, with their unwavering loyalty, martial skills, and adherence to the code of Bushido, stood prepared to protect their place of origin.

Despite their arrangements, the Japanese defenders confronted a powerful adversary. The Mongol forces unleashed a devastating assault, overwhelming some of the Japanese defenses and taking images strategic places. However, the Japanese samurai and their allies fought another time valiantly, sporting out fierce hand-to-hand combat and showing extraordinary bravery.

It become in some unspecified time in the future of the primary invasion that the legendary samurai, Suenaga Takezaki, top notch himself. His heroic exploits, chronicled inside the "Mongol Invasion Scrolls," depict his unwavering loyalty and martial prowess within the face of overwhelming odds. These scrolls function a testament to the indomitable spirit of the Japanese warriors within the path of this crucial period.

Despite their initial successes, the Mongol forces encountered unexpected demanding conditions. Unfavorable weather situations, which incorporates typhoons and tough seas, accomplished a massive function in thwarting their development. These natural phenomena, later known as "kamikaze" or "divine wind," had been seen via the Japanese as a manifestation of the gods' protection and intervention.

The Mongol forces, depleted and battered, retreated after their preliminary invasion. However, Kublai Khan remained determined to triumph over Japan and launched a 2d invasion in 1281, called the Second Mongol Invasion. This time, the Mongols assembled an excellent big stress, expected to be spherical a hundred and forty,000 squaddies, found by using a big fleet.

The Japanese, having observed out from their preceding encounters, in addition fortified their defenses. They built defensive systems, which includes fortresses and stockades, to keep away from the Mongol advances. Regional lords and samurai commanders coordinated their efforts, united in their remedy to shield their region of start.

Once once more, the Mongol forces encountered fierce resistance from the Japanese defenders. The samurai warriors, driven via the use of their unwavering loyalty and the spirit of Bushido, released daring attacks and engaged the invaders in relentless fight. The Japanese naval forces, known as the "samurai navy," skillfully deployed their ships to annoy the Mongol fleet and disrupt their supply strains.

In a fateful turn of sports activities, the divine intervention of the kamikaze yet again altered the path of records. A powerful typhoon, later named "Kamikaze," struck the Mongol fleet, wreaking havoc and inflicting large losses. The Mongol forces, battered via the typhoon and the decided resistance of the Japanese defenders, faced defeat and were compelled to retreat.

The Mongol invasions, while posing a huge risk, in the long run did now not subdue Japan. The resilience, bravery, and strategic defenses of the Japanese people emerged effective. The indomitable spirit of the samurai, their unwavering loyalty to their area of beginning place, and the strategic planning of their leaders carried out a decisive feature in repelling the Mongol forces.

The Mongol invasions left a profound effect on Japanese records. They solidified the samurai's recognition as the remaining defenders of the sector, and the kamikaze have grow to be a symbol of divine safety and country wide identification. These activities furthermore spurred improvements in coastal defense structures, maritime technology, and techniques to guard Japan's sovereignty.

Zen Gardens and Tea Ceremonies: Appreciating Aesthetics

In the serene landscapes of historical Japan, timeless traditions emerged, supplying profound opportunities for contemplation, spiritual connection, and the party of aesthetics. The paintings of Zen gardens and the sensitive exercise of tea ceremonies captivated the hearts and minds of the Japanese people, offering a gateway to tranquility, mindfulness, and the appreciation of splendor. Let us embark on a adventure to discover those cherished traditions, celebrating their enduring legacy in historical Japan.

Zen gardens, referred to as "karesansui," this means that "dry landscape," are a mirrored photo of the profound connection among nature, spirituality, and aesthetics. These meticulously designed gardens, normally determined in Zen temples, offer a seen illustration of harmony, balance, and simplicity. Through careful affiliation of rocks, gravel, moss, and punctiliously determined on flowers, Zen gardens invite contemplation and a experience of serenity.

The art work of Zen gardening originated in China and come to be later embraced and diffused through the use of Japanese Zen clergymen. It have become an vital part of Zen exercise, serving as a manner to domesticate mindfulness, stillness, and a deep connection with the natural international. Zen gardens frequently incorporate factors which embody water capabilities, bridges, and symbolic rock formations, growing a area for meditation and introspection.

The layout ideas of Zen gardens encompass the essence of Zen philosophy. The use of minimalism, empty location, and asymmetry conjures up a experience of tranquility and allows the thoughts to rest and find out inner peace. The careful raking of gravel, known as "raked styles" or "waves," symbolizes the ever-converting go along with the float of life and serves as a reminder of impermanence and the fast nature of lifestyles.

Zen gardens furthermore encompass the idea of "wabi-sabi," a complicated worldview that famous splendor in imperfection, impermanence, and simplicity. This appreciation for the imperfect and the temporary encourages a deeper connection with the natural international and a reputation of the inherent beauty discovered inside the subtle records of lifestyles.

Tea ceremonies, called "chado" or "sado," provide a profound exploration of aesthetics, mindfulness, and social concord. Rooted in Zen philosophy, the tea rite is a meticulously choreographed ritual that facilities for the duration of the schooling and serving of matcha, powdered green tea. It represents a spiritual exercising, a get together, and an artwork form multi functional.

The tea rite emerged in some unspecified time in the future of the sixteenth century, induced thru Zen Buddhism and the refinement of samurai tradition. It emphasizes concord, understand, and the appreciation of beauty inside the smallest of gestures. Every aspect of the ceremony, from the right actions of the tea grasp to the choice of tea utensils and the serene setting of the tearoom, is carefully orchestrated to create an surroundings of tranquility and mindfulness.

The tea rite embodies the ideas of simplicity, humility, and the pursuit of excellence. The tea draw close, educated inside the difficult rituals and strategies, seeks to create a region in which traffic can enjoy a 2d of respite from the outside global, connecting with their internal selves and locating serenity inside the act of sharing tea.

Central to the tea rite is the concept of "ichi-move ichi-e," because of this "one time, one meeting." This notion emphasizes the specific and quick nature of every accumulating, highlighting the importance of cherishing the existing 2d and the connections sturdy thru the rite. It reminds us of the impermanence of existence and the significance of savoring each stumble upon as a valuable and singular revel in.

The aesthetics of the tea ceremony boom to the tea utensils, the tearoom's format, and the accompanying seasonal factors. Delicate ceramic bowls, bamboo ladles, and finely crafted tea caddies are selected with meticulous care to beautify the sensory revel in and raise the appreciation of splendor.

The tea rite has deeply stimulated Japanese manner of lifestyles, inclusive of art work, structure, and the manner of lifestyles. It has stimulated the introduction of superb ceramic wares, inclusive of tea bowls and tea caddies, famend for his or her simplicity and understated splendor. The tearoom itself is designed with hobby to element, incorporating elements of natural materials, subdued sunglasses, and serene lighting to create a tranquil atmosphere.

The Golden Age of Muromachi: Ashikaga Shogunate

In the resplendent annals of historical Japan, a golden age spread out with the upward thrust of the Ashikaga shogunate, marking a length of amazing cultural, imaginative, and highbrow flourishing. Known because the Muromachi length, this period witnessed the consolidation of samurai energy, the patronage of the humanities, and the cultivation of Zen Buddhism. Let us embark on a adventure to explore the Golden Age of Muromachi, celebrating the indomitable spirit of the Ashikaga shogunate and the long-lasting legacy it left on historic Japan.

The Muromachi duration spanned from 1336 to 1573 CE, named after the vicinity of Kyoto in which the Ashikaga shogunate hooked up its seat of electricity. Ashikaga Takauji, a powerful navy chief, correctly overthrew the Kamakura shogunate, marking the begin of a modern day bankruptcy in Japanese data. Under the

Ashikaga clan's rule, Japan skilled a length of political stability, financial boom, and cultural renaissance.

The Ashikaga shogunate embraced the ideals of Zen Buddhism, which completed a vast function in shaping the cultural and highbrow panorama of the Muromachi duration. Zen teachings, with their emphasis on direct revel in and intuitive perception, located a receptive goal marketplace a number of the samurai and the aristocracy. Zen monasteries, collectively with Daitokuji and Myoshinji, have come to be centers of religious practice and cultural patronage.

The Ashikaga shoguns, referred to as the Ashikaga shogunate, exercised navy and political manage over Japan, however further they verified a profound appreciation for the arts. The shoguns and their vassals actively supported artists, writers, poets, and students, developing an environment conducive to innovative and intellectual interests. This patronage introduced about a incredible outpouring of creativity and the emergence of huge cultural achievements.

One of the defining creative forms of the Muromachi duration turn out to be ink portray, referred to as "suiboku-ga" or "sumi-e." Influenced thru Zen aesthetics, ink portray sought to seize the essence of a subject with minimalistic brushwork, the use of sunglasses of black ink on white paper to supply depth, movement, and the spirit of the undertaking. Renowned ink painters, which encompass Sesshu Toyo and Shubun, attained mastery in this artwork shape, leaving a long-lasting effect at the Japanese innovative lifestyle.

Another big innovative development at some point of the Muromachi duration become the evolution of the tea rite aesthetic, known as "wabi-cha."

Influenced through Zen philosophy, wabi-cha celebrated the beauty decided in simplicity, imperfection, and rusticity. Tea masters, together with Murata Juko and Sen no Rikyu, touchy the tea rite into an artwork shape that emphasised tranquility, mindfulness, and the appreciation of the present second.

Literature moreover flourished finally of the Muromachi length, with the emergence of exceptional works of fiction, poetry, and ancient chronicles. The 14th-century epic "Taiheiki" chronicled the tumultuous activities of the length, presenting insights into the political intrigues, samurai warfare, and the transferring energy dynamics of the time. Poetry anthologies, at the side of the "Shin Kokin Wakashu," compiled via the use of Imperial command, showcased the poetic capabilities of aristocrats, samurai, and Zen priests.

The architectural panorama of the Muromachi period witnessed the improvement of the "shoin-zukuri" fashion, characterized via the aggregate of architectural elements with the tea ceremony aesthetic. Shoin-zukuri encompassed the layout of homes, temples, and Zen meditation halls, incorporating sliding doorways, tatami mats, alcoves for showing artwork, and thoroughly crafted gardens to create an environment of refinement and tranquility.

The Golden Age of Muromachi grow to be no longer without its disturbing conditions. Internal conflicts, which incorporates the Onin War that began out in 1467, plunged the united states of a right into a period of civil strife and instability. However, amidst those tumultuous instances, the cultural and creative achievements of the Muromachi duration continued to shine, imparting solace, concept, and a experience of continuity amidst the chaos.

The enduring legacy of the Muromachi period can but be witnessed within the inventive traditions, architectural patterns, and cultural practices that keep to shape current-day Japan. The appreciation for Zen Buddhism, the refinement of progressive expression, and the pursuit of aesthetic splendor remain vital to the Japanese cultural identity.

Chapter 5: The Evolution Of Traditional Theater

In the colourful cultural panorama of historical Japan, awesome forms of theater emerged, fascinating audiences with their captivating performances and evocative storytelling. Kabuki and Noh, representing contrasting but complementary theatrical traditions, unfold out and superior, leaving an indelible mark on the location of acting arts. Let us embark on a journey to discover the evolution of conventional theater, celebrating the proper enchantment and enduring legacy of Kabuki and Noh.

Kabuki, with its flamboyant costumes, dynamic actions, and melodramatic storytelling, emerged inside the course of the early seventeenth century as a form of famous leisure. Originating from the streets of Kyoto, Kabuki theater rapid acquired reputation and developed proper right into a awesome artwork form, combining elements of dance, drama, music, and lavish stagecraft.

Kabuki performances were characterised with the aid of their colorful, large-than-existence characters, known as "kabuki onnagata" and "kabuki otokoyaku." The onnagata have been male actors who specialized in portraying lady roles, studying the art work of femininity through difficult makeup, costumes, and gestures. The otokoyaku, however, depicted male characters with heightened masculinity and theatrical aptitude.

The recollections accomplished in Kabuki drew notion from a wide shape of assets, at the side of historical sports activities, legends, folklore, and current literature. They explored subjects of affection, honor, loyalty, revenge, and the conflicts of human life. The performers, with their expressive gestures, hanging makeup, and stylized actions, added the ones narratives to life at the diploma, charming audiences with their dramatic depth.

Kabuki theater underwent severa variations in some unspecified time in the future of its history. It tailored to changing tastes, social affects, and theatrical improvements. In the Edo period, hard degree device, trapdoors, and revolving ranges had been added, improving the seen spectacle of Kabuki performances. The development of hanamichi, a raised platform extending into the audience, allowed for dramatic entrances and exits, similarly enticing the spectators.

While Kabuki catered to a broader target market, Noh theater, with its touchy splendor and religious depth, emerged as a extra aristocratic and highbrow form of theatrical expression. Originating within the 14th century, Noh theater modified into deeply inspired with the aid of Zen Buddhism, combining factors of drama, poetry, music, and dance to create a profound and meditative enjoy.

Noh performances featured masked actors who portrayed quite various characters, which consist of gods, warriors, ghosts, and everyday humans. The masks, meticulously carved and painted, conveyed a wealth of emotions and expressions. The actors, known as "shite" and "waki," hired subtle actions, stylized gestures, and haunting melodies to evoke a feel of otherworldly beauty and evoke the depths of human emotion.

Noh performs frequently drew from classical Japanese literature, on the facet of "The Tale of Genji" and "The Tale of the Heike," similarly to Buddhist and Shinto mythology. The stories explored topics of transience, the person of lifestyles, and the impermanence of existence. Noh theater, with its sparse staging, poetic language, and haunting melodies, aimed to transport the target market right right into a realm of religious contemplation and evoke a profound revel in of splendor and serenity.

Both Kabuki and Noh theater have had a protracted-lasting impact on Japanese lifestyle and the appearing arts. They have stimulated the improvement of numerous theatrical bureaucracy, which embody Bunraku puppetry and present day-day Japanese drama. Kabuki, with its dynamic power and vibrant performances, keeps to delight audiences with its superb visuals and melodramatic storytelling. Noh, with its subtle splendor and spiritual depth, remains a revered paintings shape, charming spectators with its undying splendor and profound exploration of the human scenario.

The evolution of conventional theater in historic Japan, represented thru Kabuki and Noh, serves as a testomony to the rich cultural background and ingenious ingenuity of the us of a. These theatrical traditions have a terrific time the energy of storytelling, the range of human feelings, and the exploration of profound concern matters that pass past time and vicinity.

Artistic Mastery: Ink Painting and Woodblock Prints

In the area of historic Japan, a profound mastery of resourceful expression unfold out through the captivating mediums of ink painting and woodblock prints. These innovative office work, characterised thru their incredible craftsmanship, evocative imagery, and interest to detail, captured the essence of Japanese way of life and left an indelible mark on the place of paintings. Let us embark on a journey to find out the innovative mastery of ink portray and woodblock prints, celebrating their unique appeal and enduring legacy in historical Japan.

Ink portray, called "sumi-e" or "suiboku-ga," emerged as a first rate art work shape in Japan, delivered approximately with the aid of manner of the usage of Chinese ink portray traditions. It located its expression in the cautious use of black ink on white paper, in which artists sought to seize the essence of a topic with minimalistic brushwork and masterful strokes. Ink painting embodies the ideas of simplicity, stability, and concord, celebrating the splendor of the natural worldwide and the transience of existence.

Japanese ink painters, along with Sesshu Toyo, were renowned for his or her creative mastery and their capability to deliver depth, motion, and emotion via the usage of ink. Their works frequently featured landscapes, birds, vegetation, and specific factors of nature, carried out with precision and an acute expertise of the subtleties of mild and shadow. The simplicity and abstraction of ink painting allowed for a experience of poetic ambiguity, inviting web site traffic to ponder and interpret the art work through their very non-public memories.

Woodblock prints, or "ukiyo-e," flourished at a few degree in the Edo length (1603-1868) and feature grow to be a well-known art work form some of the not unusual human beings of Japan. Ukiyo-e prints had been created via a meticulous method regarding the collaboration of artists, carvers, and printers. The prints showcased bright shades, problematic statistics, and compelling narratives, reflecting the every day lives, style, amusement, and herbal landscapes of the time.

Ukiyo-e prints often depicted scenes from the "floating worldwide" or "ukiyo," a time period used to give an explanation for the hedonistic and brief pleasures of Edo society. They captured the bustling metropolis existence, kabuki actors, adorable courtesans, landscapes, and legendary testimonies. The works of famend artists inclusive of Hokusai, Hiroshige, and Utamaro obtained large reputation, each in Japan and internationally, for their charming imagery and technical excellence.

The approach of creating woodblock prints concerned the carving of complex designs onto wooden blocks, every block representing a one-of-a-kind colour or detail of the composition. The blocks had been then inked and pressed onto paper to provide the final print. This hard paintings-widespread technique required notable functionality and collaboration between the artist, carver, and printer.

Ukiyo-e prints executed a widespread function in disseminating well-known life-style, fashion tendencies, and amusement to a big target market. They captured the creativeness of the loads, supplying glimpses into the location of pleasure districts, theater, and the natural splendor of Japan. The prints no longer exceptional showcased the imaginitive facts of the creators but moreover meditated the goals, aspirations, and desires of the humans all through the Edo period.

The innovative mastery of ink portray and woodblock prints continues to inspire artists and paintings enthusiasts spherical the vicinity. These forms of creative expression have amusing the beauty of simplicity, the harmony of nature, and the ephemeral nature of lifestyles. They embody the profound connection between paintings and existence, inviting visitors to contemplate the fleeting moments and locate solace, pride, and notion in the international around them.

The Jesuit Missionaries: Christianity in Japan

In the colourful tapestry of ancient Japan, an excellent bankruptcy opened up with the arrival of Jesuit missionaries, marking the introduction of Christianity to this historical land. This come upon among East and West, marked with the beneficial useful resource of interest, cultural change, and spiritual exploration, holds a totally precise region in Japanese records. Let us embark on a adventure to discover the Jesuit missionaries and the fascinating tale of Christianity in historical Japan, celebrating the iconic spirit of curiosity and openness.

The arrival of the Jesuit missionaries in Japan came about in the course of the 16th century, a time of massive transformation and phone with the outside worldwide. Led through the usage of the influential Portuguese Jesuit priest Francis Xavier, the missionaries sought to unfold the lessons of Christianity and establish a foothold in this far off land.

The Jesuit missionaries arrived in Japan at a time of political turmoil and moving energy dynamics. The u . S . Became divided among numerous daimyo, effective nearby lords who dominated over their domains. The missionaries, recognizing the potential to gain guide and patronage, sought alliances with influential daimyo who've been receptive to overseas mind and intrigued with the beneficial resource of the brand new understanding and generation introduced by means of the Europeans.

The Jesuits initially encountered interest and interest amongst a few segments of Japanese society. The Portuguese shoppers, who had hooked up change members of the own family with Japan, facilitated the initial touch among the missionaries and the nearby populace. The missionaries, with their statistics of Western technological knowledge, arts, and philosophy, captured the eye of intellectuals and aristocrats who have been eager to explore new thoughts and perspectives.

The Jesuits tailored their method to the community customs and cultural sensibilities, gaining have an effect on via their mastery of language, engagement in scholarly debates, and apprehend for Japanese traditions. They found the Japanese language, adopting the neighborhood dress and etiquette, and provided Christianity in a manner that resonated with Japanese values and beliefs.

One big detail of the Jesuit challenge in Japan end up their attention on education. The missionaries installed schools and delivered Western knowledge and mastering strategies to the Japanese humans. Through schooling, they sought to instill Christian values, sell literacy, and create a bridge between East and West. Some of those schools, which encompass the College of St. Paul in Nagasaki, have grow to be facilities of intellectual and cultural alternate.

Chapter 6: Feudal Lords And Strategies

In the tumultuous pages of ancient Japan's information, a monetary catastrophe of conflict, ambition, and strategic prowess unfolds—the Warring States Period. This era, known as the Sengoku length, witnessed a fragmented Japan, divided among feudal lords vying for electricity and supremacy. Within this chaotic panorama, the art of conflict and strategic brilliance flourished, shaping the future of the kingdom. Let us embark on a adventure to discover the Warring States Period, celebrating the indomitable spirit of feudal lords and their strategic acumen.

The Warring States Period spanned from the late 15th century to the overdue 16th century, a time of political upheaval and territorial disputes among effective feudal lords, or daimyo. The weakening precious authority of the Ashikaga shogunate allowed nearby lords to claim their independence and try for dominance over their opponents.

Feudal lords, pushed with the useful resource of the use of ambition, sought to enlarge their territories, consolidate their power, and constant their positions through navy might probably and strategic alliances. They employed severa strategies and processes to benefit the higher hand in this complicated interest of power, which includes diplomatic maneuvering, monetary leverage, and navy improvements.

One extraordinary parent of this period end up Oda Nobunaga, a visionary daimyo regarded for his army genius and innovative techniques. Nobunaga sought to unify Japan below his rule and employed ambitious strategies that confounded convention. He brought firearms, utilized siege conflict strategies, and displayed a eager understanding of highbrow struggle to dismantle his combatants and gain manage over strategic territories.

Another prominent discern became Toyotomi Hideyoshi, a former peasant who rose to end up one of the maximum powerful daimyo in Japan. Hideyoshi displayed exceptional army control and first-rate organizational capabilities. Through his military campaigns, he controlled to bring about a semblance of concord and balance to the struggle-torn land, laying the muse for the subsequent Tokugawa shogunate.

Strategic alliances performed a vital role in the quest for electricity during the Warring States Period. Feudal lords sought to forge alliances, create coalitions, and constant the loyalty of various daimyo. Marriage alliances, hostage exchanges, and political marriages have end up not unusual device to set up bonds and deter functionality adversaries. These alliances have been not without their complexities and shifting loyalties, as daimyo navigated a treacherous political landscape.

In addition to army would in all likelihood, feudal lords identified the significance of monetary sources and infrastructure in their pursuit of energy. They sought to bolster their domain names thru land improvement, agricultural reforms, and trade networks. Economic prosperity furnished the necessary property to maintain armies, reward dependable retainers, and finance formidable navy campaigns.

During the Warring States Period, castles emerged as strategic strongholds and logos of strength. Feudal lords built complex fortresses atop strategic locations, incorporating current protection structures, difficult architectural designs, and the cutting-edge day enhancements in citadel advent. These castles served now not handiest as protective bastions however moreover as political facilities, administrative hubs, and emblems of the lord's authority.

The techniques hired via feudal lords sooner or later of this period were no longer restrained to the battlefield by myself. They diagnosed the importance of intelligence accumulating, espionage, and subterfuge. Shinobi, skilled covert marketers and infiltrators, finished a huge role in gathering facts, sporting out sabotage missions, and executing assassinations. These shadow warriors, called ninjas, possessed information in stealth, cowl, and unconventional battle strategies.

The Warring States Period changed into characterized with the useful resource of a constant usa of flux, with transferring alliances, fierce battles, and treacherous betrayals. Feudal lords displayed fantastic resilience, adaptability, and strategic brilliance inside the face of adversity. Their indomitable spirit and unwavering strength of mind formed the path of historical Japan's information, laying the inspiration for the following unification of the usa under the Tokugawa shogunate.

Hidden Warriors: The Ninja and their Techniques

In the enigmatic shadows of historical Japan, a secretive organization of warriors emerged, shrouded in thriller and professional within the arts of espionage, sabotage, and unconventional warfare— the Ninja. These covert operatives, with their amazing talents and foxy techniques, achieved a essential role within the tumultuous history of Japan. Let us embark on a adventure to discover the hidden warriors, celebrating their legacy and the appropriate strategies that described their craft.

The origins of the Ninja may be traced over again to the medieval period of Japan, mainly at some point of the Sengoku or Warring States Period (overdue 15th to overdue 16th century). Their lifestyles is shrouded in secrecy, and historic information concerning their sports activities are often fragmented or embellished with legends and myths. Nevertheless, their effect on Japanese information and famous life-style cannot be denied.

The time period "Ninja" itself interprets to "character who endures" or "one who is hid." This aptly reflects the clandestine nature of their paintings and the vital developments they embodied—stealth, adaptability, and resourcefulness. Ninja had been frequently related to espionage, sabotage, assassination, and collecting intelligence for their employers, who have been generally feudal lords or rival factions.

One vital difficulty of the Ninja's craft become their know-how in stealth and evasion. They mastered the artwork of silent motion, allowing them to navigate thru severa terrains, infiltrate enemy territories, and gather statistics undetected. They professional notably in specialised strategies which include "silent walking" (nogare), which involved minimizing noise and leaving no hint in their presence.

Disguise and deception had been essential to the Ninja's repertoire. They employed numerous disguises and disguising techniques to combination seamlessly into their environment or infiltrate enemy strongholds. They need to redecorate their look through the usage of costumes, makeup, and mask, adopting exceptional identities to perform their missions with out arousing suspicion.

The Ninja additionally possessed a outstanding array of unconventional guns and device to resource them of their endeavors. These guns have been regularly designed with secrecy, versatility, and portability in thoughts. Examples of Ninja weapons embody the shuriken (throwing stars), the kunai (multi-motive tool and weapon), and the fukiya (blowgun). They additionally employed specific system in conjunction with grappling hooks, smoke bombs, and caltrops (spiked metallic gadgets) to create diversions or keep away from their pursuers.

The paintings of ninjutsu encompassed a massive type of abilities and strategies, both physical and intellectual. Ninja were professional in various martial arts disciplines, including taijutsu (unarmed fight), kenjutsu (swordsmanship), and bojutsu (personnel stopping). They moreover honed their abilties in camouflage, lock choosing, entice setting, and the usage of poisons. The mixture of physical prowess, strategic questioning, and unorthodox techniques allowed the Ninja to triumph over ambitious stressful situations.

The intelligence-collecting detail of the Ninja's artwork become crucial to their fulfillment. They employed a community of informants, spies, and messengers to build up statistics and relay messages covertly. They applied codes, hidden messages, and mystery hand signs to speak securely with their allies. The capability to evaluate the enemy's strengths, weaknesses, and intentions supplied a considerable benefit in making plans and executing missions.

Legends and well-known subculture have attributed supernatural competencies to the Ninja, which incorporates invisibility or control over the elements. While those money owed may be decorated, they spotlight the enduring fascination and mystique surrounding the ones covert warriors.

The legacy of the Ninja keeps to captivate the creativeness, no longer fine in Japan but across the vicinity. Their abilties, strategies, and elusive nature have permeated literature, films, and famous tradition, turning them into enduring symbols of stealth, resilience, and unconventional conflict.

The Unification of Japan: Toyotomi Hideyoshi

In the annals of historic Japan's information, a brilliant determine emerged whose indomitable spirit, strategic brilliance, and unwavering dedication brought about the unification of the nation—Toyotomi Hideyoshi. This visionary leader, born of humble origins, rose from a peasant historical past to come to be one of the most influential figures in Japanese records. Let us embark on a adventure to find out the existence and achievements of Toyotomi Hideyoshi, celebrating his pivotal function in the unification of ancient Japan.

Toyotomi Hideyoshi, to begin with named Hiyoshimaru, modified into born in 1537 in the province of Owari. He started out his life as a peasant, running in the fields and serving as a sandal-bearer for Oda Nobunaga, a effective daimyo who recognized Hideyoshi's intelligence, resourcefulness, and navy aptitude.

Hideyoshi displayed remarkable knowledge as a army strategist and speedy rose thru the ranks under Nobunaga's tutelage. He proved instrumental in diverse military campaigns, contributing to the victories that solidified Nobunaga's position as a powerful stress within the land. Hideyoshi's strategic brilliance and unwavering loyalty earned him the trust and apprehend of his lord.

After Nobunaga's untimely death in 1582, a strength war ensued, leaving a void in control. Hideyoshi emerged as a key contender in this turbulent period. With a eager information of the political landscape, he skillfully maneuvered alliances, overwhelmed rival factions, and consolidated his electricity.

One of Hideyoshi's maximum large achievements changed into the a success final touch of Nobunaga's vision of unifying Japan. He continued the efforts started out via his predecessor and launched into a series of army campaigns to convey the final domains under his control. Through his navy prowess, global own family participants, and regular pursuit of victory, Hideyoshi progressively expanded his affect for the duration of america.

Hideyoshi's campaigns have been no longer limited to brute strain by myself. He employed some of techniques to make certain success. His military improvements protected the use of firearms, advanced siege war approaches, and careful logistical planning. He recognized the significance of securing alliances, worthwhile loyalty, and selling a experience of cohesion amongst his topics.

Hideyoshi's quest for unification extended beyond army conquest. He completed severa reforms to bolster his rule and promote balance. These reforms encompassed land redistribution, the set up order of a class machine based totally on social fame, and the implementation of policies geared in the direction of controlling the strength of the samurai beauty. Hideyoshi's efforts contributed to the centralization of authority and the steadiness of the realm.

Perhaps one in each of Hideyoshi's maximum formidable endeavors changed into his strive to conquer Korea and set up a foothold in China. In 1592, he released the primary of invasions of Korea, called the Imjin War. While the campaigns to start with done significant victories, they in the long run delivered about stalemate and withdrawal. Nevertheless, Hideyoshi's ambition to growth his have an effect on beyond Japan hooked up his a long way-carrying out vision and his preference for nearby dominance.

Hideyoshi's legacy extends beyond his navy achievements. He completed a critical function in fostering cultural and financial prosperity sooner or later of his rule. He supported the arts, promoted exchange, and endorsed the development of superb castles and grandiose gardens. Hideyoshi's patronage and cultural contributions left a protracted-lasting effect on the classy and inventive traditions of historic Japan.

Toyotomi Hideyoshi's reign because the de facto ruler of Japan came to an give up together along along with his loss of life in 1598. His passing marked the start of a new chapter in Japanese facts, as strength shifted to the Tokugawa shogunate underneath Tokugawa Ieyasu. Nonetheless, Hideyoshi's unification efforts laid the foundation for a unified Japan and set the extent for the peaceful stability that could represent the Tokugawa era.

Chapter 7: Tokugawa Shogunate And The Samurai Class

In the grand tapestry of ancient Japan's records, a length of peace, prosperity, and cultural refinement emerged—the Edo Period. Lasting for over and a half centuries, this period changed into described through the rule of thumb of thumb of the Tokugawa shogunate, a centralized government that added stability and transformation to the land. At the coronary coronary coronary heart of this era stood the samurai class, an important part of Japanese society whose noble virtues and martial prowess have come to be synonymous with the spirit of ancient Japan. Let us embark on a journey to discover the Edo Period, celebrating the Tokugawa Shogunate and the respected samurai beauty.

The Edo Period, furthermore referred to as the Tokugawa Period, spanned from 1603 to 1868, encompassing the reign of the Tokugawa shogunate. It changed into a time of relative peace and balance after the tumultuous Warring States Period. The shogunate set up its seat of electricity in the metropolis of Edo (present-day Tokyo), which grew proper into a bustling town and the middle of political, monetary, and cultural existence.

Under the Tokugawa shogunate, Japan end up ruled by means of a strict hierarchical gadget known as the "bakuhan" device. At the top of this device stood the shogun, who held closing army and political authority. The shogunate maintained a employer grip on power, the use of strict guidelines and control over domains to ensure stability and prevent the upward thrust of capability challengers.

Central to the Edo Period was the samurai beauty, who served due to the fact the backbone of the Tokugawa manipulate and embodied the code of bushido— the manner of the warrior. The samurai have been the noble warriors, renowned for his or her martial prowess, concern, and unwavering loyalty. They long-established the ruling elite and had been entrusted with upholding the legal hints, preserving order, and protecting the domain names they served.

Samurai society have become characterized via way of manner of a strict code of conduct and a experience of responsibility to their lords. They had been skilled in numerous martial arts disciplines, which encompass kenjutsu (swordsmanship), kyujutsu (archery), and horsemanship. The samurai dedicated their lives to the pursuit of excellence in each army and highbrow interests, frequently undertaking calligraphy, tea ceremonies, and poetry.

During the Edo Period, the samurai magnificence experienced a shift of their position inner society. With the relative peace of the generation, many samurai located themselves transitioning from warriors to directors, students, and bureaucrats. The samurai have become the governing magnificence, answerable for overseeing their domain names, accumulating taxes, and maintaining social order.

The Tokugawa shogunate carried out hints geared toward controlling the samurai beauty and preventing functionality uprisings. The sankin-kotai system, as an example, required daimyo (feudal lords) to spend alternate years in Edo, efficaciously retaining them below the shogun's watchful eye. This machine now not exceptional ensured the loyalty of the daimyo but moreover promoted cultural trade and monetary improvement inside the capital.

As the samurai elegance superior, a great samurai manner of life emerged, characterised with the beneficial useful resource of a very particular set of values, aesthetics, and customs. They embraced the arts, literature, and philosophy, contributing to the flourishing of traditional Japanese arts which consist of Noh theater, tea ceremonies, calligraphy, and the paintings of the samurai sword.

The Edo Period additionally witnessed enormous economic and social modifications. The shogunate finished guidelines that promoted financial growth, fostered change, and installed a stable economic gadget. Towns and towns thrived as facilities of commerce, and a rich service provider beauty called chonin emerged. While below the samurai beauty in social reputation, the chonin performed a crucial function in the usage of the monetary prosperity of the generation.

However, the inflexible social hierarchy of the Edo Period confined social mobility. The 4-tiered splendor device, known as the "eternal order of the 4 training," solidified social differences between samurai, farmers, artisans, and buyers. While every elegance had its precise roles and duties, there were times of humans growing above their social recognition via knowledge, education, or remarkable achievements.

The Edo Period also noticed the isolationist insurance known as sakoku, which restricted foreign places have an effect on and make contact with with the outdoor global. Foreign change turned into in large component constrained to the port of Nagasaki, wherein the Dutch and Chinese maintained constrained circle of relatives members with Japan. Despite this insurance, cultural exchange and ingenious effect from China and Korea persisted to form Japanese aesthetics and traditions.

The Edo Period stands as a testament to the ingenuity, creativity, and stability of historic Japan under the Tokugawa shogunate. The samurai beauty, with their unwavering loyalty, martial prowess, and power of will to honor, exemplified the spirit of historic Japan and contributed to the cultural refinement that characterized the technology.

Floating World: The Culture of the Pleasure Quarters

In the colorful tapestry of historical Japan's records, a global of beauty, enjoyment, and creative expression flourished—the pleasure quarters, called the "ukiyo." These bustling districts, complete of teahouses, theaters, and satisfaction houses, furnished an break out from the restrictions of daily lifestyles and supplied a glimpse into a realm of splendor, indulgence, and diffused culture. Let us embark on a adventure to discover the captivating subculture of the satisfaction quarters, celebrating the spirit of the "floating worldwide" that captivated the hearts of historical Japan.

The way of life of the pleasure quarters reached its top during the Edo Period (1603-1868), a time of relative peace and stability under the Tokugawa shogunate. These districts, often positioned in critical cities such as Edo (Tokyo), Kyoto, and Osaka, have turn out to be vibrant centers of enjoyment and cultural trade.

One of the maximum well-known delight quarters grow to be the Yoshiwara district in Edo. Established in 1617, it rapid have end up famend as a hub of costly leisure and delicate arts. The Yoshiwara district have become meticulously designed with ornate form, lovable gardens, and a labyrinthine format that extra appropriate the texture of thriller and enchantment.

The pleasure quarters catered commonly to the prosperous samurai splendor, who sought respite from their obligations and the rigid social expectations in their positions. Within those districts, clients need to immerse themselves in a worldwide of sensitive pleasures, along with conventional music, dance, theater, poetry, and the enterprise agency of professional courtesans referred to as "oiran" or "geisha."

Geisha, specifically, performed a tremendous function within the cultural landscape of the satisfaction quarters. These as a substitute expert lady entertainers captivated their audiences with their records in numerous arts, including traditional dance, making a song, track, and witty communication. Geisha embodied grace, sophistication, and a deep knowledge of Japanese traditions, turning into icons of splendor and refinement.

The geisha's splendid appearance, characterised via their complex hairstyles, splendid kimonos, and white-powdered faces, brought to their enchantment. They were professional at attractive their customers in captivating conversations, gambling conventional musical gadgets collectively with the shamisen, and appearing elegant dances just like the "mai" or "kouta."

The delight quarters were not confined to the leisure provided via the usage of geisha on my own. The districts supplied a giant type of diversions, collectively with kabuki theater, a shape of classical Japanese drama characterized through way of its colourful costumes, exaggerated gestures, and dramatic performances. Kabuki theater showcased historical narratives, legendary recollections, and contemporary reminiscences, captivating audiences with its spectacle and emotional depth.

In addition to theater and geisha enjoyment, the pleasure quarters additionally featured tea houses in which buyers must partake within the traditional Japanese tea rite. This ritualistic exercising emphasized mindfulness, tranquility, and the appreciation of aesthetics. The tea houses inside the delight quarters served as serene retreats, presenting an opportunity for introspection and a momentary break out from the bustling international outside.

Chapter 8: Meiji Restoration And Modernization

In the grand saga of historical Japan's information, a transformative financial disaster spread out—the Meiji Restoration. This length marked a rebirth, a turning aspect that propelled Japan into the modern-day technology, in which historical traditions merged with progressive thoughts to form a kingdom poised for fast transformation. Let us embark on a adventure to find out the Meiji Restoration and the big modernization efforts that celebrated the spirit of historic Japan at the same time as embracing the winds of trade.

The Meiji Restoration commenced out in 1868, marking the cease of the Tokugawa shogunate and the recovery of imperial rule under Emperor Meiji. The restoration become pushed by way of the usage of manner of a desire to reclaim Japan's sovereignty, reestablish the electricity of the emperor, and chart a ultra-modern route for the country's future. It sought to interrupt free from the regulations of isolation and embody the enhancements of the Western global.

One of the vital issue the use of forces in the back of the Meiji Restoration changed into the selection to modernize Japan and capture up with the industrialized international locations of the West. The leaders of the recovery diagnosed that the nation needed to adapt and consist of Western technology, governance systems, and educational fashions to gather this goal.

Under the Meiji government, a sequence of sweeping reforms have been implemented to modernize Japan's political, social, financial, and military systems. The feudal beauty gadget become abolished, and a greater centralized form of presidency became mounted. Western-fashion criminal codes were introduced, along side a contemporary constitution that granted rights and duties to the residents.

Education executed a critical function in the modernization efforts. The authorities set up a complete device of public schooling, modeled after Western structures, to provide a standardized education to the population. Schools were constructed, and the curriculum emphasised technological information, arithmetic, modern-day languages, and Western knowledge. This consciousness on education laid the foundation for a quite literate and skilled personnel.

To fuel monetary boom, the Meiji government embraced industrialization and sought to construct a robust and self-enough economic machine. Infrastructure initiatives, which incorporates railways, telegraph traces, and contemporary-day ports, had been advanced to facilitate trade and transportation. The authorities supplied manual and incentives for the recognition quo of present day industries, which include textiles, mining, shipbuilding, and manufacturing.

The army underwent huge reforms as well. The samurai beauty, that have been the conventional warrior magnificence, became little by little disbanded, and a national conscription device changed into carried out. The military changed into modernized, adopting Western military strategies, schooling techniques, and era. This transformation of the army strengthened Japan's protection abilties and set the level for future growth.

The Meiji Restoration additionally witnessed a profound cultural shift. While embracing modernization, the leaders of the healing sought to hold and revitalize

Japan's particular cultural historic past. Ancient traditions, collectively with tea ceremonies, calligraphy, and traditional arts, were celebrated and promoted alongside the adoption of Western practices. This fusion of vintage and new created a first-rate cultural identification for Japan within the modern-day-day era.

The restoration generation noticed the quick adoption of Western generation, customs, and fashions. The samurai class, as quickly as mentioned for his or her splendid clothing and hairstyles, determined Western-fashion apparel, and the traditional topknots gave manner to fashionable hairstyles. The arts embraced new impacts, with painters experimenting with Western strategies and problems, and literature reflecting the changing instances.

The Meiji Restoration brought approximately profound adjustments that converted Japan proper proper right into a present day, industrialized country interior a remarkably short period. The kingdom's high-quality development and resilience for the duration of this period are a testomony to the spirit of historic Japan, which embraced exchange at the same time as cherishing its rich cultural historical beyond.

The Industrial Revolution: Western Influence and Innovation

In the big chronicles of historical Japan's history, a wave of transformation swept at a few stage in the land—the Industrial Revolution. This generation, marked with the aid of the usage of rapid technological improvements and the infusion of Western have an effect on, heralded a latest age of innovation and development. Let us embark on a adventure to find out the Industrial Revolution in historic Japan, celebrating the fusion of Western expertise and ancient traditions that shaped a country on the route to industrialization.

The Industrial Revolution reached the shorelines of Japan within the past due nineteenth century, following the Meiji Restoration and the state's embody of Western mind and generation. The Meiji authorities identified the need to modernize and seize up with the industrialized global places of the West, and as a result launched into a chain of transformative reforms.

Western have an effect on permeated numerous elements of Japanese society, from governance and training to enterprise and infrastructure. The government actively sought expertise and information from the West, inviting foreign places advisors and specialists to assist put into effect present day structures and generation in Japan.

One of the important issue regions of Western have an effect on have grow to be employer and production. The Meiji government encouraged the established order of modern-day factories and industries, introducing gadget, production strategies, and medical strategies. Textile generators, ironworks, shipyards, and mining operations emerged, using the country's commercial boom.

The adoption of Western equipment and manufacturing strategies revolutionized traditional industries. For example, the silk enterprise, already famend for its exceptional craftsmanship, embraced mechanized looms, allowing accelerated production and first-rate. Traditional crafts which includes pottery and ceramics additionally observed upgrades in manufacturing approaches and strategies.

Infrastructure improvement performed a essential role in facilitating commercial enterprise increase. The authorities launched into an ambitious software of constructing railways, roads, telegraph lines, and modern-day-day ports. These dispositions no longer most effective connected unique regions of Japan however moreover facilitated exchange, transportation, and the movement of products and people.

Education underwent exquisite adjustments at some stage inside the Industrial Revolution. The government set up a contemporary academic system modeled after Western structures, with an emphasis on technology, arithmetic, and realistic talents. Technical colleges and universities have been hooked up to educate engineers, scientists, and professional employees favored for employer improvement.

The Industrial Revolution moreover witnessed the rise of entrepreneurship and innovation. Entrepreneurs, inspired thru Western industrialists, seized possibilities to set up their personal companies and contribute to the dominion's monetary growth. They embraced new mind, superior manufacturing strategies, and delivered present day merchandise to fulfill the converting needs of society.

The Western have an impact on extended to the vicinity of shape and concrete planning. Cities underwent adjustments, with the advent of Western-style houses, widespread boulevards, and urban services. The Tokyo Station, completed in 1914, stands as an iconic photo of this period, mixing Western architectural styles with Japanese elements.

The impact of the Industrial Revolution prolonged beyond the place of employer. It brought about social modifications, which incorporates urbanization and the boom of the center magnificence. As people moved from rural regions to cities attempting to find employment possibilities, new social dynamics emerged, influencing the cloth of Japanese society.

Amidst the short modifications, ancient Japanese traditions and values remained deeply rooted. The fusion of Western knowledge and innovation with traditional information and craftsmanship created a very precise aggregate that described Japan's industrialization journey. The state embraced modernity even as cherishing its cultural history, finding a balance amongst development and preserving ancient traditions.

Samurai Spirit: Bushido in the Modern Age

In the timeless tapestry of historic Japan's history, the spirit of the samurai continues to resonate—a spirit that embodies honor, loyalty, and unwavering self-control to a code of behavior called Bushido. Though the age of the samurai has exceeded, their legacy lives on, inspiring and influencing the contemporary age. Let us embark on a journey to discover the long-lasting essence of the samurai spirit, celebrating how Bushido endures as a guiding force within the hearts and minds of the Japanese humans.

Bushido, that means "the manner of the warrior," encompassed a difficult and fast of values and necessities that ruled the behavior and mind-set of the samurai elegance. It emphasized loyalty, integrity, braveness, and strength of mind, forming the foundation of the samurai's identification and actions. These virtues have been deeply ingrained in their training, shaping them into warriors of superb skills and noble character.

Though the samurai elegance officially ceased to exist with the Meiji Restoration and the give up of feudalism, the essence of Bushido continued to permeate Japanese society and culture. Its have an impact on can be visible in severa additives of contemporary Japan, starting from agency practices and sports activities sports activities to schooling and well-known way of life.

One manifestation of the samurai spirit within the cutting-edge age is visible within the realm of business enterprise ethics and professional behavior. The requirements of Bushido, including loyalty, integrity, and honor, resonate with Japanese enterprise corporation practices, emphasizing the importance of preserving endure in thoughts, fascinating responsibilities, and adhering to a ethical code of conduct.

In the area of sports activities, the spirit of the samurai shines via in disciplines along with kendo, judo, and karate. These martial arts now not most effective awareness on bodily prowess but also instill a sense of discipline, recognize, and mental fortitude. Practitioners try and embody the ideas of Bushido each on and rancid the education mat, wearing the samurai spirit into the aggressive vicinity.

Education in Japan additionally consists of elements of Bushido, nurturing the values of vicinity, apprehend for authority, and personal integrity. Students are encouraged to increase a strong paintings ethic, to encompass challenges with courage, and to domesticate a enjoy of responsibility toward society. These requirements, harking back to the samurai's determination to self-development and societal harmony, form the character and mind-set of Japanese kids.

The effect of Bushido extends beyond conventional realms into famous manner of life, literature, and media. Numerous books, movies, and manga draw notion from the samurai ethos, portraying characters who exemplify the noble virtues of honor, loyalty, and self-sacrifice. These narratives rejoice the long-lasting appeal of the samurai spirit, fascinating audiences each in Japan and spherical the sector.

Even in times of adversity, the samurai spirit has served as a supply of notion and resilience for the Japanese people. Throughout records, the state has faced numerous stressful situations, from natural disasters to financial crises. In such moments, the principles of Bushido—courage, perseverance, and selflessness—have guided human beings and companies, fostering a experience of concord and indomitable spirit.

The contemporary-day embodiment of the samurai spirit may be seen within the enduring apprehend and reverence for tradition and historical past that permeate Japanese society. Whether thru traditional arts, tea ceremonies, flower association, or calligraphy, the Japanese humans pay homage to their cultural roots, preserving the essence of historic Japan in a converting worldwide.

Arts and Crafts: Pottery, Lacquerware, and Kimono

In the wealthy tapestry of historical Japan's cultural heritage, the humanities and crafts hold a completely unique area, embodying the meticulous craftsmanship, aesthetic sensibility, and profound cultural significance of the u . S .. Among the many resourceful traditions that have flourished at some stage in the centuries, pottery, lacquerware, and the art work of kimono stand as undying expressions of Japanese creativity and talent. Let us embark on a journey to discover the ones loved art forms, celebrating their beauty, ingenuity, and the long-lasting spirit of historic Japan.

Pottery, known as "yakimono" in Japanese, has an extended and illustrious records in Japan. From historic instances, Japanese potters have harnessed their ability to convert clay into vessels of extraordinary splendor and application. The artwork of pottery is deeply rooted in the Japanese idea of "wabi-sabi," which embraces imperfection, simplicity, and the appreciation of herbal forms.

One of the most celebrated varieties of Japanese pottery is "raku ware." Developed in the 16th century with the resource of the potter Chojiro, raku ware is characterised thru its rustic attraction, irregular shapes, and precise glazes. The firing device includes eliminating the pottery from the kiln at excessive temperatures and hastily cooling it, resulting in particular crackling and wealthy, earthy tones.

Another famend pottery lifestyle is "Hagi ware." Originating inside the town of Hagi, this style is reputable for its serene beauty and sensitive, milky-white glaze. Hagi ware embodies a feel of tranquility and ease, shooting the essence of historic Japanese aesthetics.

Lacquerware, or "urushi," represents a meticulous craft that combines natural lacquer, derived from the sap of the urushi tree, with severa substances collectively with wood, metallic, and paper. This historic art work form has been practiced in Japan for loads of years, producing notable items of unparalleled beauty and durability.

The approach of creating lacquerware includes multiple layers of lacquer being applied and polished to acquire a smooth, lustrous ground. Skilled artisans lease diverse ornamental techniques, which include "maki-e" (sprinkled image) and "raden" (inlaying shell), to embellish lacquerware with difficult styles, scenes from nature, or sensitive gold and silver designs.

The art work of kimono, the traditional Japanese garment, represents a harmonious combination of information, material artistry, and cultural symbolism. The kimono is an embodiment of Japanese aesthetics, with its elegant strains, outstanding fabric, and meticulous hobby to detail.

The manner of creating a kimono consists of weaving complex patterns, dyeing the material using strategies along facet "yuzen" (a way of hand-portray) or "shibori" (tie-dyeing), and punctiliously assembling the garment the usage of conventional sewing strategies. Kimono designs often mirror seasonal motifs, natural landscapes, or auspicious symbols, providing a glimpse into the wealthy tapestry of Japanese cultural historic past.

Each area of Japan has its non-public splendid forms of kimono, with Kyoto being mainly famend for its traditional cloth craftsmanship. In Kyoto, the paintings of kimono-making has been preserved and handed down through generations, ensuring the continuation of this loved manner of existence.

Beyond pottery, lacquerware, and kimono, historical Japan boasts a myriad of diverse inventive traditions and crafts. Woodblock printing, known as "ukiyo-e," captured the creativeness of the loads with its bright colours and specific scenes depicting landscapes, historic sports activities, and the each day lives of the human beings.

Sword-making, or "katana," represented a surprisingly esteemed craft that blended metallurgy, aesthetics, and the concepts of martial arts. Swordsmiths committed their lives to getting to know the artwork of forging blades of high-quality exquisite and beauty, with each katana turning into a testomony to the smith's potential and the reverence for the samurai spirit.

Bamboo crafts, paper-making, calligraphy, and numerous exclusive imaginitive traditions flourished in ancient Japan, every reflecting the nation's reverence for nature, interest to detail, and resolution to maintaining cultural historical past.

Chapter 9: Blossoms Of Tradition Cherry Blossom Viewing

In the resplendent tapestry of ancient Japan's cultural history, the blooming of cherry blossoms holds a unique region—a cherished way of lifestyles that celebrates the ephemeral beauty of nature and embodies the spirit of renewal and appreciation for the fleeting moments of existence. Known as "hanami," the act of cherry blossom viewing has captured the hearts and imaginations of the Japanese people for loads of years, weaving a sensitive thread that connects ancient traditions with the triumphing. Let us embark on a adventure to discover the enthralling global of cherry blossom viewing, celebrating its timeless enchantment and the iconic spirit of ancient Japan.

The way of life of hanami lines its roots lower once more to the Nara Period (710-

794), even as individuals of the Imperial Court may also want to build up below the blooming cherry bushes to partake in poetry readings, tune performances, and feasts. This exercise step by step unfold at a few stage inside the aristocracy, and in the end, it have turn out to be a cherished custom amongst humans from all walks of life.

The cherry blossom, or "sakura" in Japanese, holds deep symbolic significance in Japanese manner of lifestyles. It represents the ephemeral nature of life, the beauty of transience, and the appreciation of the triumphing moment. The blossoming of cherry wood heralds the appearance of spring, casting a spell of attraction as sensitive crimson and white petals carpet the panorama.

The hanami season commonly starts offevolved in overdue March and extends into early April, relying on the region and climate conditions. During this time, parks, gardens, and streets throughout Japan turn out to be embellished with a extensive ranging show of cherry blossoms, attracting crowds of people eager to partake on this loved manner of life.

Hanami gatherings regularly comprise family, pals, or colleagues coming together under the blooming cherry trees to have a terrific time the splendor of nature. Picnics and outside feasts are unfold out on colourful blankets, with an array of scrumptious food and drinks, which include conventional treats together with "bento" bins, sushi, and sweet rice desserts.

As the sun units, the surroundings takes on a magical amazing. Lanterns are lit, casting a soft glow upon the blossoms, growing an airy atmosphere that heightens the revel in of tranquility and beauty. Some hanami spots even provide middle of the night illuminations, permitting web page visitors to realise the cherry blossoms in a one-of-a-kind moderate.

The act of hanami is not restricted to daylight revelry. In truth, midnight hanami, called "yozakura," holds its private attraction. The illuminated cherry blossoms create a captivating sight, evoking a revel in of surprise and enchantment due to the reality the petals glow within the darkness.

Throughout information, cherry blossoms have inspired endless poets, artists, and musicians. The delicate beauty of the blossoms has been immortalized in poems, paintings, and musical compositions, turning into a supply of idea and contemplation. These innovative expressions function a testomony to the deep connection among the Japanese humans and the cherry blossom, celebrating its undying enchantment and significance.

Various sorts of cherry trees can be positioned inside the course of Japan, each with its very own precise traits. Some of the maximum famous kinds include the Yoshino cherry, which is known for its enough white blossoms, and the Somei Yoshino cherry, a hybrid range cultivated for its easy appearance and delicate perfume.

Cherry blossom viewing is not constrained to Japan alone. The beauty of those blooms has captivated human beings spherical the arena, and many nations now have their very non-public hanami fairs, inspired thru the Japanese lifestyle. This global appreciation for cherry blossoms serves as a testament to the time-honored enchantment in their sensitive and ephemeral splendor.

Geisha: The Enigmatic Icons of Traditional Entertainment

In the captivating tapestry of ancient Japan's cultural ancient beyond, the parent of the geisha stands as an enigmatic icon—a picture of grace, beauty, and subtle artistry. Adorned in top notch kimonos, with porcelain-white complexions and intricate hairstyles, geisha have captivated hearts and minds with their mastery of traditional leisure. Let us embark on a journey to get to the lowest of the mystique surrounding geisha, celebrating their particular characteristic in historical Japan's cultural landscape and the iconic appeal they keep.

Geisha, referred to as "geiko" in Kyoto and "geigi" in precise areas, are expert entertainers who deliver interest to traditional Japanese arts including dance, song, poetry, and communique. Their origins can be traced lower back to the

18th century, at the identical time as female performers referred to as "tayuu" entertained guests in delight quarters. Over time, geisha evolved into super and pretty expert artists, embodying the epitome of touchy splendor and cultural sophistication.

The training to become a geisha is rigorous and worrying. Young women, referred to as "maiko," commonly start their education in their early young adults, entering an okiya (geisha residence) in which they stay and study under the steerage of an skilled geisha, known as the "okasan" or "mother." The training length lasts numerous years and entails learning numerous conventional arts, studying the complicated rituals of tea ceremonies, and growing subtle social abilties.

One of the distinguishing abilties of geisha is their terrific apparel. They are regularly seen sporting lavish kimonos adorned with complicated styles and colorful solar shades, carefully selected to reflect the seasons or unique sports. The artwork of dressing as a geisha calls for precision and hobby to element, with layers of undergarments and add-ons meticulously organized to benefit an extremely good ensemble.

Geisha are also appeared for his or her one-of-a-type hairstyles. Elaborate arrangements of the hair, adorned with decorative hairpins and accessories, are crafted to complement the geisha's appearance and kimono. These hairstyles are taken into consideration works of artwork in themselves and require expert hairstylists to create and maintain.

Geisha are masters of traditional Japanese appearing arts. They undergo huge education in numerous disciplines, along with dance, music, creating a music, and instrument gambling. Their performances display off a persevering with combination of grace, precision, and diffused artistry, transporting audiences to a global of beauty and beauty.

Ochaya, or tea houses, feature the number one venues for geisha enjoyment. These institutions offer an intimate setting wherein site visitors can enjoy the company of geisha on the equal time as being entertained with the beneficial useful resource in their performances. Geisha are professional conversationalists, attractive visitors in witty banter, storytelling, and video video games, all brought with impeccable grace and appeal.

The international of geisha is shrouded in mystique and etiquette, with strict codes of behavior and social protocols. They adhere to a fixed of professional ethics known as "geisha-do" or "the manner of the geisha," which emphasizes loyalty to their customers, discretion, and keeping the very pleasant requirements of professionalism. Geisha are professional for his or her thoughts, wit, and capability to navigate social situations with grace and poise.

Contrary to well-known false impression, geisha are not courtesans or prostitutes. They are performers and entertainers who're deeply dedicated to preserving and promoting traditional Japanese manner of existence. The feature of a geisha is to offer a sophisticated and cultured environment, unique visitors via their innovative abilities and appealing verbal exchange.

The geisha lifestyle has confronted traumatic situations over the years, particularly inside the course of durations of social and cultural trade. However, the spirit of the geisha endures, as they keep captivating audiences and keeping the paintings paperwork that outlines historical Japan. Today, geisha keep enchanting traffic at special activities, conventional ceremonies, and cultural gala's, making sure the continuation of this cherished manner of lifestyles.

Chapter 10: The Island Beginnings

Can you listen the echoes of statistics? The whispers of the beyond carried on the wind during the majestic mountains, rolling hills, and coastal plains of Japan. Let's dial the clock again, way over again—approximately 16 thousand years—to the Jomon length, the dawn of Japanese civilization.

Picture this: A group of humans toughened with the useful useful resource of the uncooked power of nature, reputation at the expensive land surrounded with the aid of manner of infinite blue seas their hair thick and wavy, their eyes alert and curious, and their hearts brave and adventurous. These have been the Jomon humans, the real population of Japan. They were hunter-gatherers, residing in harmony with nature, their life marked via the usage of manner of the seasonal rhythm of lifestyles.

The Jomon period, named after the twine-markings at the pottery produced in the course of this period, is one of the earliest regarded examples of pottery inside the international. Imagine palms, roughened with the beneficial useful resource of exertions and climate, shaping clay into vessels, carving complex patterns inspired by manner of nature. Each pottery piece, a testomony to the human spirit, all of the time taking snap shots a second in their life, a slice in their tale.

Figure 2 Dogu in Jomon Period

The maximum iconic decide of this period is the 'Dogū', mysterious clay collectible collectible figurines often characterized by way of manner in their bulging eyes and curvaceous our our bodies. Were they talismans, toys, or deities? We can also by no means virtually recognize, however their enigmatic presence reminds us of the rich cultural tapestry woven via the Jomon human beings.

Fast in advance to spherical 300 BC, and we are in the Yayoi period. Our diploma: a scene of rice paddies stretching closer to the horizon, an orchestra of lifestyles orchestrated by the seasons. Rice cultivation had been delivered from the Korean Peninsula, marking a essential shift from a hunter-gatherer society to an agrarian one. A exchange so profound, it would all the time adjust the landscape of Japan—every honestly and figuratively.

The Yayoi human beings, further to their pottery, additionally left at the back of one-of-a-kind exciting artifacts, which includes the dotaku. These bronze bells, adorned with complex designs, trace at the growing sophistication of the society. Were they used for rituals, or as a photograph of reputation? While the right use stays a thriller, their existence factors to an more and more complicated society.

At the coronary coronary heart of this alteration turn out to be the fame quo of primitive social instructions, giving rise to chieftains and the concept of authority. These early stirrings of based totally society, but minuscule, had been the number one threads of a tale that would cause the stunning tapestry of emperors, shoguns, and samurais.

While the ones durations may moreover seem remote and precis, echoes of the Jomon and Yayoi cultures are even though located in modern-day Japan. From pottery gala's that honor the craft of the Jomon, to the Yayoi-inspired agricultural practices and fairs celebrating the rice harvest, the ones historic periods left an indelible mark at the Japanese psyche.

So, as we depart the misty beaches of prehistoric Japan, we feature with us a deeper knowledge of the those who first known as those islands domestic. A society that started out with pottery and primitive device, developed into rice cultivation and metallurgy, and step by step unique the bedrock of a way of life, a civilization, that would hold to thrive and evolve for millennia to return. The tale of Japan is clearly starting, and as we flip the pages, the narrative best gets extra charming. Ready to delve deeper?

As we sail faraway from the Yayoi length, a extremely-modern-day sunrise breaks on the beaches of Japan, marking the advent of the Asuka and Nara periods. It's right here, amidst the mild rustling of bamboo and the lyrical chirping of cicadas, that the classical age of Japan starts to unfurl.

The Asuka duration, spanning from 538 to 710 AD, modified right into a transformative technology for Japan. This modified into the age wherein the winds of trade carried with them a ultra-modern spiritual philosophy from the mainland - Buddhism. It changed into Prince Shotoku who welcomed those winds, and with them, the seeds of Buddhism. Picture him, a leader with a imaginative and prescient, someone of serenity amidst the turbulence of electricity struggles.

Figure three Prince Shotoku

Prince Shotoku modified into no longer most effective a proponent of Buddhism, however additionally a visionary who sought to reform Japan's governance primarily based definitely mostly on Chinese fashions. His Seventeen-Article Constitution, a protracted manner from a modern-day-style charter, became extra of a moral and political education, putting the tone for a centralized authorities and promoting Buddhist values. The echoes of his in advance-wondering thoughts can no matter the truth that be heard in the standards of harmony and recognize that underpin Japanese society in recent times.

As the Asuka period makes way for the Nara length, the canvas of history gets even greater vibrant. The Nara length, which extended from 710 to 794 AD, noticed the blossoming of Buddhism and the flourishing of subculture. It is all through this era that the capital moved to Nara, an architectural wonder modeled after Chang'an, the Tang Dynasty capital of China.

Imagine the metropolis of Nara in its complete glory: grand Buddhist temples, elegant aristocratic mansions, busy markets, and the bustling hubbub of metropolis existence. At the coronary coronary heart of this town stood the Todai-ji, a massive Buddhist temple housing the Great Buddha, an awe-inspiring bronze statue that stays a wonder to within the interim. Constructing the Todai-ji changed into no easy feat, eating maximum of Japan's bronze manufacturing and nearly bankrupting the united states of america. But the temple stands, a testament to the grandeur and energy of the technology and a photo of the large have an effect on of Buddhism on Japanese society.

In the quieter corners of the Nara duration, far from the imposing temples and bustling town existence, the seeds of Japanese literature commenced to sprout. In the court docket, noblewomen penned their evaluations and feelings, culminating in works just like the "Man'yoshu", an anthology of poetry, and "Kojiki", an account of historic Japanese facts and mythology.

It's within the Man'yoshu where we meet Kakinomoto no Hitomaro, one of the most notable poets of the time. His eloquent expressions of love, loss, and the transience of lifestyles echoed the human sentiments of the generation, leaving an indelible mark on Japanese literature.

The Nara period isn't pretty much the grandiosity of its form or the eloquence of its literature, although. It's moreover about the profound transformation of Japan's society and subculture, pushed through the effective strain of Buddhism and political reform. From the commands of Prince Shotoku to the grandeur of the Todai-ji temple, the effect of this classical era continues to ripple through time, forming a essential part of Japan's cultural DNA.

So, as we close to this monetary wreck and depart at the back of the classical age of Japan, we stock ahead a story formed via non secular transformation, political reform, cultural blossoming, and human sentiment. We're beginning to see the various threads that make up the tapestry of Japanese data, and as we preserve our adventure, those threads will intertwine in increasingly tricky and captivating patterns. Onwards, then, to the next chapter in our journey thru the annals of Japan's facts.

Chapter 11: The Imperial Influence

As we step into the Heian period, spanning from 794 to 1185 AD, we are greeted thru an air of sophistication, a enjoy of sensitive splendor. This is a realm wherein poetry flows like water and artistry is as ample because the cherry blossoms in spring. And at the heart of all of it is the radiant imperial court docket docket of Heian-kyo, present day-day Kyoto.

The first element you need to recognize about the Heian length is that it became a time of excessive cultural development, a duration that many don't forget the peak of Japanese aristocratic way of lifestyles. Picture the Heian court docket docket: an area of colorful shades, state-of-the-art style, and touchy tastes. But, in all likelihood mainly, it have come to be an area of intrigue, in which political power modified into regularly acquired or misplaced in the whispers of the courtiers.

Enter Fujiwara no Michinaga, a person who embodied this complicated dance of power. Michinaga become not an emperor, but he also can as well were. As a member of the powerful Fujiwara extended family, he deftly maneuvered his daughters into imperial marriages, ensuring his control over the throne. His difficult, chess-like video video games of electricity offer a charming perception into the mechanisms of political maneuvering inside the imperial court docket.

Figure 4 Fujiwara no Michinaga

Yet, the Heian length became not satisfactory about political maneuvering. This come to be additionally an generation of tremendous literary output. If we pay attention closely, we're able to pay interest the whispers of the 'Pillow Book', wherein Sei Shonagon, a court docket female, pens down her observations, musings, and courtroom gossip. Then there is 'The Tale of Genji' with the aid of the usage of Murasaki Shikibu, often taken into consideration the area's first novel. This story of affection, loss, and political intrigue gives us a window into the world of the Heian courtroom like no special.

Meanwhile, inside the realm of faith, Buddhism continued to comply. The Tendai and Shingon sects, brought with the resource of Saicho and Kukai respectively, have grow to be influential, introducing complicated rituals and esoteric teachings. If you have ever big the vibrant and complicated mandalas in a Japanese temple, you've got witnessed the enduring legacy of those practices.

Yet, amidst this flourishing lifestyle and religious improvement, a cutting-edge day elegance became growing, simmering at the outskirts of the courtroom's radiance - the samurai. Their rise come to be a response to the remote and disinterested court, which have turn out to be often oblivious to the conditions within the some distance off provinces. The samurai, to begin with provincial warriors, ought to eventually become a power that couldn't be left out, putting the extent for the tumultuous eras to return once more.

So, as we depart the Heian duration, we take with us memories of political intrigue, literary masterpieces, and the beginnings of the samurai's rise. As a good deal as it have become a time of cultural flourishing, it became additionally a duration of political decline, developing a evaluation as interesting because of the truth the length itself. It's this juxtaposition, this duality of cultural height and political decay, that makes the Heian length such a compelling economic wreck in Japan's records.

As we turn the internet internet web page and journey ahead, we are going to see how this fascinating period laid the foundation for the dramatic epochs to come back lower back. Hold tight, because we're heading into the technology of the samurai, a time of bravery, loyalty, and fierce strength struggles. The dance of Japan's history keeps, each step more fascinating than the remaining.

The Samurai and Shoguns

As the curtain falls on the Heian period, we see the putting solar glistening off the blades of the samurai, the navy nobility who would probable come to rule Japan for over seven hundred years. Let's soar into the riveting epochs of Kamakura, Muromachi, and Azuchi-Momoyama durations, a tumultuous era of samurais, shoguns, and incessant electricity struggles.

First save you: Kamakura, 1185 to 1333 AD. This era have come to be christened with the popularity quo of the Kamakura shogunate with the useful useful resource of Minamoto no Yoritomo, the number one shogun. Think of the shogunate as a army dictatorship, with the shogun ruling the roost. This was a seismic shift from the Heian length, shifting the political center a ways from the illustrious court docket docket docket and firmly into the fingers of the samurai.

Figure 5 The Samurai

Let's zoom in on the Mongol invasions of 1274 and 1281, in which we discover the Kamakura shogunate going thru its excellent take a look at. The Mongols, led thru the formidable Kublai Khan, tried to subjugate Japan, best to be repelled instances, aided with the aid of manner of typhoons - famously referred to as 'Kamikaze' or divine winds - which ravaged the Mongol fleets. Although the shogunate had held business enterprise, the rate of protecting the land may want to eventually contribute to the Kamakura shogunate's downfall.

Cue the doorway of the Ashikaga extended family, instigating the Muromachi duration, from 1336 to 1573 AD. The Ashikaga shogunate, in spite of the fact that missing the iron-fist manipulate of its predecessor, determined the bloom of culture, together with the tea rite, Noh theater, and Ikebana - the artwork of flower arranging - which keep to outline Japan's cultural identity.

But the volume emerge as set for conflict, and the Onin War (1467-1477) left Kyoto in ashes and the u . S . A . Splintered into warring states, a time referred to as the Sengoku length. This epoch have come to be rife with strength-hungry daimyos or feudal lords, each eager to capture manipulate.

In the midst of this chaos, three unifiers emerge, placing the extent for the Azuchi-Momoyama period. Oda Nobunaga, an formidable warlord, initiated the unification way. Known for his strategic prowess, he delivered lots of Japan under his control before assembly an untimely forestall within the Honnoji Incident, a coup led thru one in every of his private generals, Akechi Mitsuhide.

But the unification emerge as a protracted way from over. Enter Toyotomi Hideyoshi, Nobunaga's dependable retainer who avenged his lord, defeated Akechi, and finished the assignment of unification. Hideyoshi, a person born of humble origins, could climb the ladder to the peak of strength, a testament to the opportunities and brutality of the Sengoku period.

Yet, even Hideyoshi's reign turned into now not to remaining. After his loss of life, his unswerving exceptional pal, Tokugawa Ieyasu, seized manage, establishing the Tokugawa shogunate which could probable final for over 250 years, a story for our next financial ruin.

Through the narrative of samurais and shoguns, we're able to see the transformation of Japan from an imperial courtroom to a land ruled via warriors. This technology, at the same time as punctuated via battle, additionally saw the flourishing of subculture and the shaping of the Japan we apprehend these days. It's a fantastic reminder that splendor and brutality can exist aspect with the aid of aspect, similar to the samurai - a fierce warrior and a consumer of arts. This duality, this intertwining of war and manner of life, remains a defining detail of the narrative of Japanese facts.

Chapter 12: The Closed Kingdom

As we keep our journey, we discover ourselves in a land of contrasts, wherein peace and isolation make an uneasy alliance. Welcome to the Edo period, an era that spanned from 1603 to 1868 and is often remembered for 2 terrific additives: the reign of the Tokugawa shogunate and Japan's national seclusion policy, referred to as Sakoku.

Following the turbulence of the Warring States period, the country craved tranquility and order. Tokugawa Ieyasu, the primary shogun of this era, supplied that. The Tokugawa shogunate dominated for over 250 years, reaching an remarkable period of balance and peace in Japanese records.

Let's talk about Edo, now known as Tokyo. Under the shogunate, Edo transformed from a sleepy fishing village to considered certainly one of the biggest towns in the global, a bustling epicenter of tradition and alternate. Edo way of life, because it got here to be said, became marked with the useful resource of great styles of theater like Kabuki and Bunraku, the popularization of Ukiyo-e, or woodblock prints, and the emergence of Haiku as a mainstream poetry form.

Yet, it have turn out to be additionally an generation of isolation. Fearful of the unfold of Christianity and remote places impact, the shogunate applied Sakoku, a policy that critically restricted foreign places get entry to and Japanese departure. With the exception of a few controlled shopping for and selling posts, like Dejima for the Dutch, Japan remained a global apart.

A international apart, but no longer a international behind. Sakoku provided an uncommon ecosystem wherein Japanese way of life must evolve without direct distant places have an effect on. The america superior, albeit at its very very own rhythm, turning inward to foster a excellent life-style and societal shape.

Imagine a society meticulously compartmentalized into four primary schooling: Samurai, Farmers, Artisans, and Merchants. This inflexible hierarchy, stimulated with the useful resource of Confucian principles, have become a defining feature of the Edo period. Intriguingly, irrespective of their position at the bottom of the social ladder, investors often accrued wealth, a paradox that chafed towards the social norms of the time.

Now, meet Basho Matsuo, a figure emblematic of this era's rich cultural tapestry. A draw near of Haiku, Basho imbued this smooth however profound form of poetry with the essence of Zen and the temporary beauty of nature, a concept known as "Mono no Aware." His verses mirror the era's introspective bent, underlining the depths Japanese manner of existence plumbed for the duration of its isolation.

Figure 6 Basho Matsuo

Peppered in some unspecified time in the future of this era had been moreover times of revolt and dissent, maximum drastically the Shimabara Rebellion, led by means of manner of Christians in opposition to oppressive taxation. It emerge as brutally suppressed, and its aftermath similarly solidified the shogunate's resolve to place into effect Sakoku.

Ironically, Japan's self-imposed isolation become breached through the very forces it sought to preserve at bay. When American Commodore Matthew Perry arrived together along with his 'Black

Ships' in 1853, stressful Japan open its doors to the outdoor international, the sun started out to set on the Edo period and the Sakoku coverage.

In retrospect, the Edo period offers a charming have a have a study of the way a society can improvement in isolation, preserving peace and fostering a unique manner of lifestyles. Its profound impact is plain in contemporary Japan, from bustling Tokyo, a nod to the thriving Edo, to the long-lasting attraction of Kabuki and Haiku. As we step into the subsequent bankruptcy of our journey, we discover a Japan on the point of giant transformation, teetering among way of existence and the tantalizing attraction of the present day worldwide.

The Meiji Restoration and a New Dawn

Imagine this: it is 1868, and an archipelago tucked away within the jap corner of Asia is teetering on the edge of big transformation. The solar rises on the Meiji technology, marking the surrender of the Tokugawa shogunate and the graduation of a duration that would redefine Japan all the time.

The Meiji Restoration, because it came to be seemed, wasn't best a political overhaul; it have come to be a revolution of idea, tradition, and society. One of the most defining elements grow to be the transfer of strength from the shogunate returned to the Emperor, the more youthful Meiji Emperor, who came to symbolize the today's, modernized Japan.

Yet, in the back of this reputedly peaceful switch of electricity modified into a tide of discontent, upheaval, and conflict known as the Boshin War. The clans of Choshu and Satsuma, as soon as considered rebels, led the revolution in the direction of the shogunate, eventually installing location a brand new government beneath the Meiji Emperor.

The leaders of the Meiji era had a completely unique imaginative and prescient: "Fukoku Kyōhei," or "Enrich the us, make more potent the navy." They believed that to protect their sovereignty from Western powers, Japan needed to embody the very component it had resisted during Sakoku - Western information and technology.

Fast-beforehand to 1872, and the primary railway line is inaugurated amongst Tokyo and Yokohama. Imagine the excitement, the surprise, and in all likelihood a touch of apprehension because the Japanese human beings witnessed a locomotive thunder in some unspecified time in the future of their region of start for the first time. It wasn't handiest a marvel of engineering; it have grow to be a photo of the rapid pace of alternate.

Westernization permeated every element of life. The conventional samurai topknots gave way to western hairstyles, the kimono to the western suit. Even the historical capital of Kyoto grow to be changed with the useful resource of Edo, now renamed Tokyo, symbolizing the shift in the path of a greater Western-centric international order.

Yet, the Meiji technology come to be not pretty a whole lot copying the West but amalgamating the amazing of each worlds. Education, for example, saw a synthesis of Western notion and Japanese values. The advent of obligatory training in 1872 became a huge step, supporting to shape a society that valued literacy and getting to know.

During this period, Japan moreover promulgated its first constitution, aptly named the Meiji Constitution, and installation a bicameral parliament, the

Imperial Diet. These developments were not without their worrying situations, but they set the diploma for the u . S .'s burgeoning democracy.

On the other side of this coin turn out to be the save you of the samurai beauty. The 1876 Haitōrei Edict forbade samurai from carrying swords, marking the forestall of an era. Many samurai discovered new professions, while a few, unable to clearly take delivery of the exchange, sparked rebellions, the maximum well-known of which have become led with the aid of manner of Saigo Takamori, the "closing actual samurai."

The Meiji generation have grow to be also a time of cultural blossoming. Take, for instance, the works of Lafcadio Hearn, furthermore known as Koizumi Yakumo. A Greek-born author who made Japan his domestic, Hearn's writings added Japanese folklore and legends to the Western international, maintaining Japan's cultural ancient beyond amid the sweeping tide of modernization.

The Meiji technology, which lasted until 1912, set Japan on a course from feudalism to modernity. It became a length of unparalleled change that laid the idea for Japan's later successes and traumatic conditions. It served due to the fact the bridge between the vintage and the trendy, all the time converting the course of the kingdom's information. As we delve into the subsequent chapters, we are able to see how the seeds sown at some point of this period may additionally form Japan's adventure inside the 20th century.

The Rising Sun I

Picture a bustling Tokyo within the Nineteen Twenties. The metropolis, as fast as a feudal capital, is now a colourful metropolis with western-fashion houses, a bustling railway device, and citizens walking approximately in each conventional kimono and Western suits. Welcome to the Taisho generation, a significantly short but pivotal 2d in Japan's facts, wherein democracy bloomed and way of life thrived.

The Taisho technology (1912-1926) could have been short, but it changed into long on have an effect on. The phrase "Taisho" manner "brilliant righteousness," and it added a shift from the antique Meiji oligarchic authorities to a more democratic tool. This have emerge as the era of "Taisho Democracy," in which the energy of the Imperial Diet grew, and the impact of civilian control began to enhance.

Now, allow's meet Hara Takashi, who've grow to be the first commoner appointed as Prime Minister in 1918. His upward push signaled a wreck from the manner of existence of military and court docket docket docket the Aristocracy dominating Japan's control, reflecting the democratic spirit of the instances. Though his tenure changed into reduce brief with the aid of an murderer's blade in 1921, his legacy of promoting extra inclusive politics marked a tremendous shift in Japanese society.

The technology's democratic ethos moreover stirred a cultural revolution called the "Ero, Guro, Nansensu" (Erotic, Grotesque, Nonsense). This cultural movement, an exploration of the absurd, the beautiful, and the sensual, have become a rebellious reaction to the short modernization and Westernization of society.

The Twenties moreover witnessed the proliferation of cafes, movie theaters, and jazz golf equipment in Japan, in particular

Tokyo's Ginza district. A particular fusion of Western and Japanese sounds emerged, and Nippon Jazz changed into born, with performers like Ryoichi Hattori most important the wave.

The cultural effervescence prolonged to literature, with this period giving rise to prominent authors like Akutagawa Ryunosuke, Japan's "Father of the Short Story," and Natsume Soseki, who, a laugh fact, have become the face of the one thousand yen phrase until 2004. Their writings pondered the complex interaction of conventional Japanese values and Western thoughts.

But due to the fact the pronouncing is going, each silver lining has a cloud. The Great Kanto Earthquake of 1923 became a catastrophe that left Tokyo and Yokohama in ruins, causing large devastation and lack of existence. It modified into a stark reminder of nature's power amid the heady improvement of human society.

As we transition from the Taisho era into the early Showa length, we discover a Japan at crossroads. The loss of lifestyles of the Taisho Emperor in 1926 and the ascension of Emperor Hirohito marked the start of the Showa technology, "Showa" translating to "Enlightened Peace."

The early Showa generation is a tale of evaluation. It witnessed a continued fascination with Western way of life, resulting in a "Modern Girl" (Moga) phenomenon, wherein younger women sported bobbed hair and quick skirts, smoked cigarettes, and cherished purchaser lifestyle. This have become a time at the same time as cinema flourished, with directors like Yasujirō Ozu and Kenji Mizoguchi developing movies which is probably now professional as classics.

However, on the turn side, financial crises similar to the Showa Financial Crisis (1927) and the global Great Depression (1929) hit Japan hard. Rising unemployment, tough work movements, and civil unrest marked those turbulent times.

Increasing militarization commenced out to eclipse the spirit of democracy. By the Nineteen Thirties, Japan commenced its march inside the path of a course of competitive growth, which sooner or later caused the darkish days of World War II. This aspect of Japan's data is a reminder of the way societal currents can extensively exchange the route of a state.

Looking again, the Taisho and early Showa periods were full of superb contrasts - enlightenment and disaster, cultural flourishing and military ascension, democratic advances and authoritarian impositions. This dichotomy is a important part of statistics Japan's complex historic and cultural material. As we skip in advance, we are going to delve into how the ones tensions performed out inside the most devastating of methods sooner or later of the shadows of war.

Chapter 13: The Shadows Of War

As we delve into the Showa period's darkish coronary heart, it is vital to preserve in thoughts that history isn't in reality an workout in recounting records. It's a tale of people, their triumphs, and their screw ups, their hopes, and their fears. The story of World War II in Japan isn't always any special.

Imagine taking walks the streets of Tokyo in the Nineteen Thirties, a town divided. You'd see army parades showcasing Japan's developing navy may additionally additionally on one hand, on the same time as cafes and jazz golf equipment although hummed with modern-day-day music and more youthful strength on the alternative. The Japanese Empire end up flexing its muscle mass, but the shadow of what become to return again hung inside the air like a darkish shroud.

The narrative of WWII in Japan started with a miscalculation. Japan, caught within the grip of a fierce military-commercial enterprise force, discovered resource-rich lands to its south as the panacea for its economic ailments. The infamous invasion of Manchuria in 1931 set the level, however it modified into the overall-scale incursion into China in 1937 that certainly introduced Japan's competitive intentions to the arena.

One can't neglect about the frightening incident of the Nanking Massacre for the duration of the Sino-Japanese battle, wherein tens of hundreds of harmless civilians suffered unspeakable atrocities. This darkish episode of Japanese army aggression is a stark reminder of the devastating effects of struggle on humanity.

Japan's involvement in WWII have grow to be legitimate with the bombing of Pearl

Harbor on December 7, 1941, a date President Roosevelt declared would "live in infamy." This audacious assault stunned the united states, propelling them into a conflict that turn out to be already raging in some unspecified time in the future of Europe and Asia. From that 2nd on, Japan decided itself embroiled in a battle of not viable scale and devastation.

But amidst the grimness of war, there had been humans whose moves left a profound impact. One such man or woman have become Chiune Sugihara, a Japanese diplomat stationed in Lithuania, who defied his authorities's orders and issued transit visas to masses of Jewish refugees. His act of defiance, driven via compassion, stored round 6,000 lives, earning him the pick out "Japan's Schindler."

As the warfare raged, every day lifestyles in Japan have come to be an increasing number of harsh. Resources have been scarce, with human beings enduring excessive rationing and living beneath steady fear of air raids. Propaganda and censorship have been rampant, controlling the narrative and stoking nationalist fervor. Despite the hardships, the human beings persevered, hoping for a better destiny.

The tragic quit result of WWII for Japan came in August 1945 with the atomic bombings of Hiroshima and Nagasaki. The overwhelming destruction and absence of existence brought via "Little Boy" and "Fat Man" - the reputedly danger loose names given to the atomic bombs - were no longer like some thing the arena had seen. The haunting photograph of the Hiroshima Peace Memorial, or Genbaku Dome, though reputation amidst the large destroy, serves as a solemn reminder of this catastrophic occasion.

In the days following the bombings, on August 15, 1945, Emperor Hirohito made a radio broadcast saying Japan's give up. This was the number one time the Japanese public had heard their Emperor's voice, a second etched within the collective reminiscence of the Japanese humans.

The quit of the conflict marked a seismic shift in Japan, with a rustic left to grapple with the aftermath of extremely good destruction and the profound experience of loss. Yet, even in those dire situations, the indomitable spirit of the Japanese humans continued. The seeds of restoration had been already being sown, and as we're going to see in our subsequent financial disaster, the ones would in all likelihood go through fruit in strategies that few have to have imagined.

To nowadays, the reminiscences and instructions of the conflict deeply have an effect on Japanese society, subculture, and its pacifist charter. The Showa technology changed into certainly a time of contrasting extremes, embodying each the darkest shadows and the brightest lighting fixtures of Japanese records. But like a phoenix, Japan would upward push from the ashes, setting itself on a direction to recovery, peace, and prosperity. But that is a tale for our next bankruptcy.

The Phoenix Rises

In the aftermath of World War II, Japan grow to be a kingdom reduced to rubble, its cities devastated, its people demoralized, and its financial machine shattered. The Land of the Rising Sun decided itself in darkness, but like a phoenix, Japan would upward thrust from the ashes, demonstrating an awe-inspiring story of resilience, tenacity, and transformation.

In the early post-struggle years, Japan have become occupied through Allied forces, led via america. Under the everyday steering of General Douglas MacArthur, amazing political and social reforms took root. The maximum distinguished many of the ones emerge as the drafting of the publish-struggle charter, all the time etched in Japanese records due to the fact the 'Postwar Constitution' or 'Constitution of Japan.' This constitution, implemented in 1947, basically converted Japan's governance, setting up democratic standards and enshrining the concept of pacifism in Article 9. It moreover demystified the position of the Emperor, redefining it as a photo of countrywide harmony, in preference to a divine authority.

Life at some degree in the early publish-struggle years was tough. Scarcity became the norm, however the Japanese people confronted those hardships with strength of mind and style. One might also need to see street-factor stalls or yatai, precursors to present day colourful street meals culture, shooting up in positioned up-struggle Japan as a way of survival and network crew spirit.

In this landscape of conflict and preference, severa human beings came to the fore, their stories illuminating Japan's direction in the direction of recuperation. Take, as an example, Momofuku Ando, a person of humble beginnings, who observed a rustic hungry and in need. His response? Instant ramen. A easy, an awful lot less steeply-priced, and easy-to-prepare dish that now not handiest fed a enhancing state but also can waft on to emerge as a worldwide phenomenon.

The years of American career triggered 1952, and the level grow to be set for Japan's resurgence. Through a insurance of country-guided market economic system, Japan centered its efforts on rebuilding its enterprise base. The authorities, business enterprise, and tough work shaped a robust triad that catapulted Japan onto the area diploma as an monetary superpower. This length, extending into the 1980s, is referred to as the "Japanese monetary miracle."

This length of immoderate economic boom changed into no longer with out its quirks. The Hula-Hoop craze of the Nineteen Fifties is a fun testomony to this. It all commenced even as a toy employer called WHAM-O added the easy plastic hoop. Its popularity in Japan turn out to be incredible, becoming a picture of the kingdom's developing consumer way of existence.

Japan's ascent to technological manage have come to be marked through the upward thrust of giants like Sony, Toyota, and Nintendo, whose progressive products reached each nook of the globe. From the long-lasting Sony Walkman that revolutionized private audio to the cherished Nintendo gaming structures that added us to Mario, those products pondered Japanese ingenuity and a determination to incredible and innovation.

As Japan rose, it additionally started out to reflect on its past. An critical cultural development in some unspecified time in the future of this era become the installed order of the Hiroshima Peace Memorial Park and Museum, constructed to commemorate the lives misplaced in the atomic bombing. The annual peace ceremonies held at Hiroshima and Nagasaki became crucial to Japan's identification as a peace-loving usa.

As the 20 th century drew to a close to, Japan modified proper right into a extraordinarily one-of-a-type u . S . A . From the simplest that had emerged from the wreckage of WWII. It had no longer best recovered however had converted into an financial and technological powerhouse. Yet, this dramatic upward push become not without its challenges, and Japan needed to grapple with a transferring international landscape, evolving societal issues, and the need for further transformation within the twenty first century.

So, as we put together to reveal the final pages of this ebook, we are able to explore current Japan, navigating its brand new statistics and looking inside the direction of the future. But it certainly is a story for the following financial disaster.

Japan Today and Beyond

The final some years of the twentieth century marked the surrender of Japan's put up-conflict economic growth, and with it came new challenges and opportunities. This duration, known as the Heisei technology, started in 1989 with the ascension of Emperor Akihito, marking a brand new section in Japan's journey, one marked with the resource of way of financial trials, societal shifts, and the continuing evolution of its feature on the arena diploma.

The Heisei era began out on a somber word, as Japan grappled with the burst of the financial bubble. The subsequent duration of stagnation, referred to as the 'Lost Decade', observed deflation, elevated unemployment, and slow monetary boom. Yet, in spite of these hardships, Japan's economic machine remained actually one of the most important inside the international, showcasing the kingdom's enduring financial resilience.

Throughout this era, a series of people and improvements emerged, symbolizing Japan's adaptability and technological prowess. Perhaps no determine better embodies this than Masayoshi Son, the charismatic leader of SoftBank. His journey from immigrant to tech titan is a testomony to Japan's evolving entrepreneurial spirit.

In the arena of culture, this era also noticed Japanese famous culture, or 'Cool Japan,' take the arena via way of storm. From manga and anime to J-pop and fashion developments like Harajuku fashion, Japan's have an impact on prolonged a long way past its beaches, developing a huge imprint on worldwide famous subculture.

However, it wasn't truly economic and cultural shifts that defined the ones many years. Natural failures played a pivotal feature too. In 1995, the Great Hanshin

Earthquake, one of the deadliest in Japan's records, struck Kobe, causing massive devastation. Then, in 2011, the Great East Japan Earthquake and subsequent tsunami introduced approximately a catastrophic nuclear coincidence at the Fukushima Daiichi Power Plant.

The Fukushima catastrophe introduced Japan's dating with nuclear energy into sharp hobby. With the triple meltdown at the power plant, Japan modified into pressured to rethink its electricity regulations and has considering that made big strides in renewable strength tasks.